Dr Tony Fernando is a practising psychiatrist and sleep specialist in Auckland. He was a senior lecturer and multi-awarded teacher in psychological medicine at the University of Auckland for two decades. Tony has a PhD in compassion and has been incorporating the Buddha's teachings into his own life and work as a doctor for the past 20 years. He has received four temporary ordinations as a Buddhist monk in the Burmese tradition.

LIFE HACKS
FROM THE
BUDDHA

LIFE HACKS
FROM THE
BUDDHA

Dr Tony Fernando

HarperCollins*Publishers*

Names and details of case studies mentioned in this book have been changed to preserve anonymity.

HarperCollins*Publishers*
Australia • Brazil • Canada • France • Germany • Holland • India
Italy • Japan • Mexico • New Zealand • Poland • Spain • Sweden
Switzerland • United Kingdom • United States of America

First published in 2024
by HarperCollins*Publishers* (New Zealand) Limited
Unit D1, 63 Apollo Drive, Rosedale, Auckland 0632, New Zealand
harpercollins.co.nz

A catalogue record for this book is available from the National Library of New Zealand

ISBN 978 1 7755 4239 1 (paperback)
ISBN 978 1 7754 9270 2 (ebook)
ISBN 978 1 4607 3775 0 (audiobook)

Cover design by Darren Holt, HarperCollins Design Studio
Cover images by istockphoto.com
Typeset in Bembo MT Pro by Kirby Jones
Printed and bound in Australia by McPherson's Printing Group

MIX
Paper from
responsible sources
FSC
www.fsc.org   FSC® C001695

For my compassionate mother, my beautiful seven siblings, my caring partner and the numerous Buddhist teachers and practitioners who taught me the Buddha's hacks

CONTENTS

There should be more to life

As a psychiatrist, I diagnose and treat mental illnesses such as depression, anxiety, psychosis and addiction. As a sleep specialist, I identify and treat various sleep disorders such as insomnia, nightmares, sleepwalking and sleep apnoea. For me, as a doctor, focusing solely on identifying and treating medical problems is not enough. Many of my patients get relieved of their psychiatric or sleep symptoms but their lives remain unhappy. I feel that part of my role as a doctor is to help my patients experience more meaningful and happier lives.

Early in my career as an academic at the University of Auckland, I became interested in the psychological health of medical students. Most, if not all, of our medical students are accomplished academically. Many of them have also done well in sports or the arts, and most of them are amazing human beings. They are so amazing that if I applied for medical school now, I don't think I'd get in because the competition is so stiff.

It surprised me, therefore, early on in my time as a teacher at medical school, when I became aware of how much misery and unhappiness there was among our students. Anxiety, depression, and substance abuse were rife. There was also an epidemic of perfectionism and pathologic levels of self-hatred. As a teacher, I wanted to offer more than just teaching them psychiatry, so I became interested in the research on positive psychology.

Positive psychology is the scientific study of living meaningful lives and experiencing positive emotions. I started to attend conferences in New Zealand and overseas on the topic and met some of the great scientists in the field, including Professor Martin Seligman, the person who started this psychological revolution.

As a positive psychology practitioner, I learned the power of developing gratitude through the use of a gratitude diary. I also learned to identify my strengths and move away from focusing on my weaknesses.

Around the same time, I became acquainted with mindfulness meditation. This came about when some of my severely ill psychiatric patients learned how to regulate their destructive emotions through mindfulness courses. I realised that if my patients felt better in themselves through the practice of mindfulness, I should learn it too.

I benefited from positive psychology and mindfulness practice. However, I still felt that there was something missing. There did not seem to be a coherent approach to what would help humans, like me, deal with unending stress, unease and dissatisfaction. Somehow, I felt that the various positive psychological approaches I was using to experience a happy life were piecemeal and fragmented. That is until I became acquainted with the teachings of the Buddha.

Growing up in the Philippines, which is majority Catholic, there were only two Buddhism-related things I was familiar with. First, not far from my ancestral home in old Manila, there was an exotic-looking, bright red building with a tall fence topped by dragons. I was told it was a Buddhist temple. Second, I heard whispers of a scandal when one of the girls from my sisters' Catholic school left the church and became a Buddhist. Those two things combined to create all I knew about Buddhism.

The first time I became acquainted with some of the Buddha's teachings was in 2004, six years after I finished my training in psychiatry and sleep medicine. I was browsing in a bookstore at Sydney airport when the book *The Art of Happiness* caught my attention, not because it had the Dalai Lama's smiling picture on its cover but because it was co-written by a psychiatrist, like me. For the book, American psychiatrist Howard Cutler interviewed the Dalai Lama, the spiritual leader of Tibetan Buddhists, about stress, anxiety, suffering, inner peace and happiness. I didn't know much about Buddhism, but I decided this might be a fun read as it involved a psychiatrist asking tough questions of the Dalai Lama. Little did I know that the book would change the course of my life.

Introduction

Occasionally, in life, we have a smooth stretch then – *boom!* – we hit a pothole, or worse, despite our careful driving, someone crashes into us. Thankfully, the Buddha is here to help. When our trip in this life gets bumpy, we can make it smoother, not by paving all the roads perfectly, but by installing a set of shock absorbers in the form of a series of life hacks provided to us by the Buddha.

I consider the Buddha the smartest psychologist to have ever lived. He has profound understanding of why we suffer and experience stress. Instead of blaming everyone else around us, he invites us to look inside our minds and see how our delusional tendencies complicate our situations.

His teachings made so much sense to me that I decided to ordain as a temporary monk in Burma in order to dive into the whole Buddhist experience. My experiences as a temporarily ordained Buddhist monk have been priceless, as they have given me an intimate understanding of his teaching within a Buddhist environment.

To help his followers experience less stress, the Buddha set out a training programme that consisted of understanding the nature of the mind and following a suggested way of living with others.

Apart from mindfulness, he gave practical techniques to manage our constantly chattering mind and develop wholesome qualities like generosity, living simply, honesty, integrity and compassion, all of which result in unconditional contentment and peace.

What sets apart his teachings is that they are not to be believed and followed blindly. They are not commandments or insights revealed by a superior or heavenly being. Instead, he invites us to find out for ourselves if his hacks are helpful or not. If his teachings do not suit us, then we are welcome to discard them.

How many teachers have you met who have told you to discard their teachings? This is the total opposite of what I often hear from other teachers: 'Believe and convert! Otherwise, you'll get roasted in some eternal barbeque!'

As a scientist, the approach where a hypothesis or theory is tested and solutions are found appeals to me a lot. It was a relief to be given a choice on what to believe rather than blindly believing, which is entirely different to my experience of faith-based religions. Because Buddhism does not rely on having faith in a god or supernatural being, it is often viewed as an untraditional religion.

Not only have I benefited from his teachings for the past 20 years, I have also incorporated many of his pearls of wisdom into my work as a psychiatrist and educator. Evidence of their power can be seen in the former medical students, who are now senior doctors, who have made a point of thanking me for the Buddhist life hacks I taught them more than a decade ago. I've even had inmates I taught Buddhist meditation to at Mt Eden prison tell me they found his hacks useful. One prisoner told me that after learning how to manage his thoughts, his frequent panic attacks, which were triggered every time the heavy steel doors shut, went away.

To make the Buddha's teachings easy to understand, I've used my own experiences and those of many people I have met. That said, all the clinical examples have been modified and anonymised to preserve privacy. I've also incorporated relevant neuroscience and psychology studies to show that the Buddha's teachings from 2600 years ago are only recently being validated by hard science.

This book provides a summary of the Buddha's hacks for managing life's stressors. Hacks are creative or out-of-the-box ways to solve a problem. In this instance, their purpose is the attainment of peace and happiness and the minimisation of suffering. While many of the Buddha's hacks are creative ways to get to understand and get around our crazy ways of thinking, some of them are practical life tips.

You don't have to be a Buddhist to appreciate these hacks – although some Buddhists might learn a few tricks along the way! If you are Christian, Muslim, Hindu, Jewish, of another faith, agnostic, or even an atheist, the core teachings of the Buddha on managing stress and suffering will not threaten your belief (or lack thereof). If you practise many of the hacks here, the most likely outcome is that you will be a kinder and calmer person than you were before.

In this book, I've chosen to cover the Buddha's core teachings, which are understandable and practical. Many of his other teachings are so advanced and complicated that I've deliberately stayed away from them. I have a simple mind, so I've just stuck with what I consider to be the essential and practical teachings for an easier life.

Our journey through these life hacks will start by recognising that all of us want to be happy. Though we occasionally get gratified, we are never fully satisfied. We always want more, and inevitably something always goes wrong. When this happens, the Buddha shows us that we can choose between grasping onto experiences, pleasures and ideas that – if we are unable to let go of them – cause us more stress and suffering, or we can condition our minds to be more peaceful and content.

In order to help guide you to find the peace you seek, I have summarised the Buddha's teachings into the following points:

1. All of us experience stress regardless of who we are, our health, our wealth, possessions, relationship status, profession, or surroundings. We need to stop blaming everyone or our surroundings for stress.
2. We have innate mental processes that cause us stress. To manage stress, we need to know and experience how our mind creates it.
3. Because we live in groups and communities, we need to behave in a way that will not cause harm to others. This leads to a peaceful environment, which is conducive to peace.
4. There are mental practices that will promote peace and happiness. These include generosity, mindfulness, living honestly, simply and with integrity and acting with kindness and compassion.

The Buddha

Before I talk about the Buddha's teachings on stress and happiness, let me briefly outline who he was – or perhaps, who he wasn't. The Buddha is not a god who wants to be worshipped or believed in. He was as human as you and me. Though not a god, I reckon that he is the smartest psychologist and teacher of human behaviour who has ever lived. He had incredible understanding of what causes stress, unease and dissatisfaction in humans. He also suggested (not commanded) a systematic educational training programme for happiness, peace and contentment. His approach was not based on us believing what he taught, but on his students personally understanding and experiencing the causes of stress and how his proposed training system relieves it.

The Buddha, known as Siddharta Gautama, was born in the sixth century BCE in part of northern India that is now known as Nepal. The Buddha's mother died right after his birth, so he was raised by his aunt and his father, who was the ruler of their clan. He lived a very privileged life. His father protected him from the sufferings of normal life by surrounding him with luxury and sensory pleasures. He was highly educated and was expected to follow in the footsteps of his father and become a ruler. Despite his comfortable surroundings, Siddharta was curious about the world. He felt that there was more to living a life than the pursuit of luxury and comfort.

At 29, he left his luxurious surroundings to seek mental clarity. Despite having learned from various religious teachers, he felt that he hadn't learned enough. After six years of spiritual searching, he sat under a tree to meditate until he found enlightenment. During that period of meditation, he experienced profound realisation of what causes suffering and how to achieve perfect and unconditional happiness. It was then that he became known as the Buddha – the awakened one. He is considered 'awake', because most of us are asleep to the true natures of stress and happiness.

After his deep realisations, he spent his life teaching and travelling until he passed away at the age of 80.

A community of the Buddha's disciples consisting of monks, nuns and ordinary people grew and spread throughout India. His teachings eventually reached many parts of Asia including Bhutan, Thailand, Myanmar, Laos, Vietnam, Sri Lanka, China, Mongolia, Tibet, Korea and Japan. Now, some 2600 years later, his teachings continue to influence around 500 million people who identify themselves as Buddhists. In the west, there are also millions of non-Buddhists who practise meditation techniques taught by the Buddha.

Teachings of the Buddha

This book provides only a small summary of the Buddha's teachings. To put it in perspective, the Buddha's original teachings, called the Pali canon, consists of 42 volumes, which was written down nearly 500 years after his death. Those 42 books of teachings were written over 45 years and consist of 84,000 teachings. Of these, 82,000 came from the Buddha and 2000 from his disciples. In contrast, the Christian Bible is around a quarter of the length of the Pali canon and was written by around 40 authors over at least 500 years.

As a psychiatrist, I have used more Buddhist psychological principles in helping my patients manage stress and suffering than I have western psychological approaches from Freud, Jung or Beck. I also use many of his hacks daily to manage my own life. Inspired by the Buddha's teachings on kindness, in 2012

I embarked on a PhD studying compassion, which I completed in 2021.

After close to two decades of using Buddhist techniques in my personal and clinical life, I decided to write this book so that other people might benefit as well. The Buddha teaches us how to hold things lightly, so may your life be less bumpy after learning a hack or two – or 50!

CHAPTER 1

The pursuit of happiness

We live on planet Earth, a beautiful blue and green rock that is revolving around a star in the Milky Way galaxy, one of probably 100–200 billion galaxies in the observable universe. Everything within the universe is composed of matter and energy that is always in flux, always changing, moving and dynamic.

On Earth, the tectonic plates on which we stand are constantly shifting. Mountains, oceans, the wind, the clouds are always on the move. At an organism level, our bodies are composed of constantly moving atoms and subatomic particles. At a macro level, we age, we get sick, we get better, then we get sick again and, after a few decades, we turn into decomposing matter, which gets broken down to finer particles.

The same can be said of our minds and emotions. They are always in flux. Get a raise? You are happy. Get stuck in traffic? You are angry. Get home and see your children? Your heart flutters. Notice the mess they've made? You're frustrated. And it is not just you! Everyone around you is in flux too; everything is impermanent, unstable.

Yet, we all want to be happy. No one wakes up in the morning wishing for a miserable day ahead. If we examine what we do from the moment we wake up until we go to sleep, *everything* we do is geared towards feeling good and avoiding pain and suffering.

Even when we perform mindless tasks, our motivation is always the same – we want to feel good and avoid suffering. A lot of what we do might not feel good or pleasurable at the time, but the ultimate aim of our actions is to earn some reward. This reward might come later in the day, week, month, year – or even a few years later.

I brush my teeth because I do not want the pain of rotten teeth. I drive my car because it is more comfortable than taking public transport or walking. I exercise because I feel better when I am relatively fit. I try to eat healthily because I want to be healthy and delay the aging process. (However, occasionally, I treat myself with a bag of corn chips or a salted caramel ice cream because they make me feel happy, even if it is only temporarily!)

When it comes to more immediate happiness we have access to so many things that should make us happy – we should be in the epicentre of a happiness explosion. From a sensual pleasure angle, all sorts of delights are right there at our fingertips. From my phone, I can order my favourite Thai fried noodles, Cantonese crispy pork, or a giant hamburger with every available topping. If the weather is cold, I can turn on the heater. If it is muggy, I can turn on the air-conditioning. When I am tired, I can lie on a super-comfortable mattress designed for astronauts. When my muscles are tense, I can sit on a massage chair.

We have smartphones in our pockets that can entertain us, that allow us to communicate with loved ones continents away, that provide addictive games and give us the latest news from anywhere in the world. Alcohol and recreational drugs of various types are easily accessible. Many of us travel to places some of our grandparents could never have dreamed of visiting. Our health is better and our lifespans are getting longer by the year. Our annual incomes have grown exponentially. In many western countries, sexual pleasures are no longer taboo and sexual fantasies can be fulfilled legally without the fear of being jailed, persecuted, or stoned to death. Despite regional wars going on in different parts of the world, most countries are experiencing unprecedented continuous peace.

We should be happier, right?

Despite the myriad things available that should make us happier compared to people a generation or two ago, our happiness levels have not increased. Sadly, the reverse seems to be happening. Rates of depression, anxiety, substance abuse, eating disorders, suicide, stress and burnout are all climbing. A 2023 report produced by the Centers for Disease Control research showed that around 10 per cent of American teens had attempted suicide in 2021, while 30 per cent were depressed and a third were abusing drugs, and 57 per cent of teenage girls felt constantly sad or hopeless.

Sally

Sally is what many would consider the epitome of success. She owns a successful global online company. She also recently sold one of her companies for millions of dollars after only a few years of operation. She owns houses around the world. Her kids go to boarding school and are all doing well. Her husband works with her, and their relationship is good.

On the morning of our first appointment, her secretary rang to inform me that Sally was running late as she was coming from the airport. This was understandable as it was a Monday morning so traffic was heavy. I was surprised when Sally made it to her appointment on time. Instead of driving, she'd taken a helicopter from the airport, which cut her travel time by half. When I first saw her, I was distracted by a huge diamond that hung around her neck.

She had come to see me because she was having severe problems falling asleep. She felt something was not right. Despite all her achievements, she felt that nothing gave her genuine happiness. She felt good when she made her first million, but she wanted more. She was amazed by the business awards she'd won but the satisfaction each one gave her was brief. She was happy her children were doing well in school, but she knew that in a few years' time, they would leave her. She had begun to wonder why her husband stayed with her. Was he hanging on to her mainly because of her money?

Sally is afflicted with a condition the Buddha called 'dukkha', a universal dissatisfaction, pervasive discomfort or discontent in life. Sally is not alone in her experience. Most of us are not as accomplished as Sally but all of us feel a certain level of dissatisfaction or unease with our lives. When things seem right, that feeling of contentment or comfort doesn't last – even for me. All of us experience dukkha.

Recently, I went on a dream holiday that I'd been looking forward to for almost a year. I went to Bangkok for four days and stayed in a nice hotel, but after a while I felt bored and wanted to move on. I went to cosmopolitan Tel Aviv, then to an ultra-Orthodox neighbourhood in Jerusalem. From there, I went to Salamanca in Spain where I'd enrolled in an intensive Spanish-language course that I'd wanted to do for many years. After that, four of my eight siblings, a brother-in-law, niece and nephew joined me in Madrid, and we went to Seville in the middle of that city's fantastic Easter Week celebrations. A few of us went to Morocco and even rode camels and slept in the Sahara. We stayed in palaces and had a personal guide and chauffeur for a week. It was an incredible experience being with family, enjoying all the food, the fascinating experiences and the shopping. And yet...

I longed for the calm of New Zealand and sleeping in my own bed. I got annoyed by living out of a suitcase, and I missed my partner and my routines.

After six long weeks, I flew back to New Zealand. I was happy to be home, with my partner, my comfy bed and my predictable schedule. Before long, though, I noticed myself complaining about work, thinking about how food in Spain was more exciting than in New Zealand and reminiscing about how Spaniards are livelier than Kiwis. Soon, I was planning for my next big trip.

I am not that different from Sally. She had 'everything', and I lived a traveller's dream for six weeks – but nothing was enough. Something was just not 100 per cent right.

In the core of our human experience, regardless of our situation, this constant feeling of unease and dissatisfaction exists. As I've mentioned, the Buddha called this 'dukkha'. In our current language, we call this stress.

Self-reflection

Being as honest as you can, think about a time of your life when everything seemed perfect. It might be your wedding day (or the day of your divorce), an unforgettable date, the best meal you've ever eaten, the day you got your first paycheque, the day you took possession of your first house, or the day your sick child was discharged from hospital.

Now think about how long that amazing feeling lasted. Was it minutes, hours, or days?

How long did it take before your mind focused on something else that needed to be done?

How long after your wedding did you start bickering about the bills that had piled up from it?

How long after your unforgettable honeymoon did you have to unpack your bags and face that pile of washing?

How long after that amazing meal did you start to feel queasy because you'd eaten too much?

How long after your child was well again did they start being an annoying brat?

Our good feelings never last, so we continually chase them moment by moment. This is dukkha.

The wild dog

The Buddha and his disciples once saw a wild dog run out of the forest. It stood still for a while, then it ran into the underbrush and then out again. It ran into a hollow in a tree, then out again. It went into a cave, only to run out again. It stood for a minute, then ran, then lay down, then jumped. Running was uncomfortable so it would stop. Standing was uncomfortable so it would lie down. Then it would jump up again, running into the bush, then the tree hollow, never staying still.

The wild dog blamed standing for its discomfort, then it blamed sitting, running and lying down. It blamed the tree, the underbrush and the cave. However, the wild dog had mange, which is a nasty skin infection.

We are like the wild dog. We always seek to find comfort and happiness. If we are not happy, we always blame external situations for causing stress and dissatisfaction. The problem does not always eventuate from outside of us. As it did with the dog, the problem comes from within us. We are never satisfied. There is always unease. Something is just not right. Even when things are 'perfect', sooner or later, there will be unease. This is dukkha.

This story was recounted by Ajahn Chah, one of
the foremost Buddhist masters from Thailand.

Stress

In his teachings, the Buddha approached stress the way a doctor diagnoses and treats an illness. First, he diagnosed his own experience of stress and suffering, then he concluded that *all* of us experience stress and suffering. However, the Buddha never said that all our life will be continuous stress. We experience joy, happiness and pleasure, but they are never permanent and stable.

Whether you are young, middle aged, or old, you experience stress. Whether you are a Buddhist monk, a hermit, a church bishop, or an atheist, you experience stress. The only time we do not experience stress is when we are dead, but even this is uncertain if there is such a thing as an afterlife.

What causes stress?

The Buddha was clear about what we do that causes us stress, suffering and dissatisfaction – we cling, attach or *grasp*. To me, the word grasp is visual, visceral and physical.

Grasp what? We hold tightly to expectations, possessions, what we think will make us happy or whole, and to what gives us pleasure. On a more subtle level, we grasp on to ideas, concepts, routines and the concept of 'this is me and mine'. The process of grasping, clinging and tightly holding not only causes stress, but it has also led to fights, wars and genocide.

If everything around and within us is impermanent, constantly changing and unreliable, it does not make sense to hold on to things or grasp them. It is illogical to believe that the house you spent your lifetime savings on will always be sturdy. It will need repairs and regular maintenance to be liveable. You cannot be 100 per cent certain that it can withstand an earthquake or a cyclone. So, grasping at the idea that the house will still be there in the future is illogical and the cause of stress.

The same principle applies to your body. Despite the thousands of hours we spend exercising, putting on make-up, undergoing cosmetic procedures and gulping costly supplements, we will age, get sick and turn to dust. Grasping on to our youth to try to stop aging is absurd.

Unfortunately, it also applies to relationships. I detest fairy tales that fool our children into believing that they will meet their Prince Charming or Sleeping Beauty and that they will live happily ever after. That is both aspirational and delusional. Instead, we should teach our kids that relationships can be so much fun, but that they can also cause angst and despair.

Relationships are fundamentally unstable as they are between humans who are constantly both changing physically and emotionally. Relationships require a lot of effort, kindness and understanding from all parties to make them workable and sustainable – and eventually, all relationships end through separation or death. It sounds morbid, but that is the truth. If we delude ourselves and grasp on to people who make us feel good, we are bound to be disappointed. Everything is impermanent.

The Buddha was clear that grasping causes stress. He identified the things that we grasp, which cause stress, suffering and dissatisfaction. We grasp on to the experience of certain states (for example, pleasure, comfort or fame), which we think will lead to happiness and fulfilment. We also grasp states in order to escape aspects of life that are painful, unpleasant and uncomfortable. We grasp on to:

- physical pleasures
- ideas and routines
- our preoccupation with 'I, me or mine'.

Hack 1: Physical pleasure and material possessions can only bring so much good feeling. They do not last long and can even cause complications in your life.

If we grasp tightly to feeling physically comfortable, making sure we are pain- or ache-free and sitting comfortably, after a few minutes, we will experience some mild discomfort or an urge to change positions. If instead of grasping, we accept that being comfortable is great but that it will not last, we are at peace. When we feel some urge to move and be more comfortable, we do not get angry at our chair. It has nothing to do with the chair, as our body will always eventually feel unease.

Food also brings us physical pleasure. For me, eating sushi at the fish market in Tokyo is a highlight of any trip to Japan. For a long time, no matter where I ate sushi, I expected the rice to be perfect, the fish to be fresh and the rice–fish ratio correct. I grasped on to the physical pleasure of what sushi in Tokyo could deliver. So, every time I ate sushi in New Zealand, I was disappointed and became a little cross. I expected Tokyo-standard sushi and Auckland-standard sushi was just not good enough. Even though the Auckland sushi makes a lot of New Zealanders happy, I suffered because of my attachment or grasping to what I thought the taste and texture should be.

Grasping on to physical pleasure also includes our attachment to material possessions. Many of us are deluded into thinking that the more possessions we have, the happier we become. Advertisers know this and capitalise on our weakness to desire more and more objects. We want a bigger house, a faster car, a nicer watch, or a more expensive bag. Once we have obtained what we were hoping would make us happy, we move on to the next object in a never-ending process of acquisition.

I am guilty of this. I have always liked leather bags, possibly because when I was a kid, my grandmother had many beautifully crafted ones. For a long time, I collected leather bags. Some years ago, I dreamed of buying a beautiful Ferragamo bag. I felt something indescribable when I would run my hands over the nice, soft, Italian leather. I believed that this bag would be the last one in my collection, as it cost a fortune.

One morning, while out walking in New York, I needed to go to the toilet so I headed to Saks Fifth Avenue department store. After my brief bathroom stop, some hidden force pushed me towards the leather bag section. There, an incredibly effective Irish salesman named John sold me the Ferragamo bag of my dreams. I justified the purchase by telling myself that I work hard, and I do not have a lot of expensive vices. Walking out of the shop, I felt ecstatic.

On the subway home, I hugged my bag tightly. I was worried that it might get scratched by a random person on the train. When I got back to the apartment, I stared at the most beautifully crafted bag I had ever had. This bag was supposed to make me feel good, but it did not. Instead, I became anxious that it would get scraped or damaged or stolen.

The following day, I returned the bag to Saks Fifth Avenue and immediately felt relief. At least I can say I owned the bag of my dreams for 24 hours and, for a short period, it did bring me a bit of happiness and excitement, but not the prolonged happiness I thought it would give me.

Since then, I've slowly whittled away my collection and have given some of my precious Italian bags to friends and relatives. In a weird way, there is a sense of liberation.

Hack 2: If you use the word 'should' a lot, check your stress levels and those of the people around you.

We love our ideas about how things *should* be done. I have ideas on how the Buddha's teachings should be taught, how the Bach

Cello Suites should be played, how children should behave in restaurants and how governments should be run. Lots of shoulds!

I'm sure you have ideas on how people should drive on a highway, how people should dress for parties, or how someone should make the perfect omelette.

There is nothing wrong with having our own ideas and routines. It is part of being human to have opinions and ways of doing things – we are creatures of habit. However, we get into strife when we grasp on to ideas so tightly that we do not listen to others' opinions.

'This is how you should stack a dishwasher!'

'Western-style democracy and free-market economics should be imposed on the whole world.'

'Everyone should embrace our faith and damn the non-believers.'

When we grasp on to our ideas and how things should be done, tension and conflict arises. We lose sight of the fact that even our own ideas and routines have changed through the years. Remember impermanence? How sure are you that the precious opinions you are willing to die for now will remain the same in the next few years?

While at medical school, I became very involved in a conservative Catholic group. I was going to church daily and confession weekly. At that time, I believed that Catholicism was the only way to eternal life and everyone else would be going to hell. My belief was so fervent that if the pope had called for a Holy War, I would have gone straight to Rome ready to die for the church. I was a Catholic extremist!

That was a few decades ago, and those beliefs I grasped have significantly changed, but, to a certain extent, I can relate to extremists who are willing to give up their life for their faith. They are totally absorbed in an idea. I have been there.

Self-reflection

How many times have you had arguments over ideas and philosophies?

Have you lost friends and family members over disagreements about religion or politics?

During election times in the Philippines and in the US, my family and friends have unfriended people on social media who were on the other side of the political divide. I remind my family and friends that they are giving up relationships over politicians who really do not care about them. It is the grasping on to a political belief that is the problem.

At a global level, many current and past conflicts have been driven by people who are extremely attached to their view of the world. They have grasped ideologies to the point of slaughtering millions of people who believed differently or who are perceived to be different.

In contrast, one of the most successful global empires, which lasted for 600 years with relative peace, was the Ottoman Empire. Apart from being a strong military force, the Ottomans were famous for justice and tolerance. Though the rulers and majority of the population were Muslims, Christians and Jews were allowed to practise their religions as long as they followed rules and paid taxes.

Grasping on to ideas and beliefs can cause stress and suffering not just at a personal level but also in terms of relationships and wider communities.

I am not suggesting that you give up your ideas, philosophies, routines and conventions. However, remember impermanence and that everything is in flux. There are eight billion other people with different ideas and routines out there.

· ·

Hack 3: Try not taking yourself too seriously.

· ·

'I, me or mine' is a reference to our preoccupation with the self, and learning to loosen our grasp on it is one of the most complex topics I've encountered in Buddhism.

However, I have been lucky to have met incredible teachers who have simplified the topic for me. One of them is Ajahn Sucitto, a senior English monk of the Thai Forest Tradition. He said, 'Tony, we just put too much importance on who we are. This causes suffering.'

It is not unusual for most of us to think that the world revolves around us. We should be listened to. We should be taken seriously. We should be respected. We should be happy.

Where did those delusional statements come from?

An alternative to those 'should' statements is, 'It would be nice to be listened to or taken seriously or respected. But that will not happen all the time and I will be okay.' That is an example of loosening the grasp on the concept of the self.

Despite our achievements, our looks, our family name, or the prestigious school we went to, we are just one of eight billion people made of a temporarily coalesced organic material, that breathes (for now) and desires to be respected and taken seriously.

Even though you think that you are special, it is inevitable that someone will not give you the attention or respect that you think you deserve. Your kid might ignore you. A colleague at work might say your suggestions are stupid. Your boss might not give you the pay rise you feel you are entitled to. Your partner might say that you are a jerk.

The more we think highly of ourselves, the more chance we will get hurt because of our unrealistic expectation of others and of the world. However, if we do not take ourselves that seriously, attacks on the self will not be that painful. They might even be funny!

A friend's mother was lamenting that she had developed breast cancer. She was so angry at God because she did not deserve this. She was a devout believer who followed all the rules. She was a good person who made countless donations to charities. She did not drink alcohol or use drugs. How dare God give her cancer?

I kept my mouth shut as I thought I would get a tongue lashing if I told her that her having cancer probably had nothing to do with God, and being human – and impermanent – means that our bodies will eventually get sick. I certainly wouldn't dare comment that we have a 100 per cent mortality rate.

While that might sound callous and uncaring, I was truly sympathetic to her situation, but I disagree with the entitlement that inevitably caused her extra suffering on top of the cancer.

Another favourite teacher of mine, Ajahn Brahm, says that there is nothing wrong when we get sick. Getting sick is 'right' given the nature of our bodies. To be sick is just to follow the law of nature. Of course, with technology and science, we can delay sickness a bit, but not permanently. Getting angry and blaming the universe or some supernatural entity does not help.

Jeremy

An unhealthy attachment to our self-image can lead to disastrous consequences. Jeremy owned a successful chain of stores in the US. He attempted suicide after disgruntled employee made a complaint to the tax department, alleging that Jeremy had made dishonest claims regarding his taxes for many years. The allegation was driven by anger and did not have any objective basis.

The complaint could easily have been defended, but since a potential investigation was humiliating and would tarnish Jeremy's reputation as a businessman and pillar of the community, he decided that it would be better to be dead than have his name sullied. Fortunately, his attempt failed and, through therapy, he learned how to manage his unrealistic attachment to his image and reputation.

Hack 4: Many of our thoughts are like soap bubbles, they are empty. Do not grasp on to them.

Apart from taking ourselves too seriously, we also take our thoughts too seriously. When we think of something, we often think of it as true: 'I think it, therefore it is true!'

For many of us, when we have a particular worry or concern – for example, 'I might fail in my exam' – we view it as a normal worry and, as long as we prepare well, the chances of it happening are slim.

But for overthinkers or ruminators, when a worry comes on, they grasp on to the worry like a dog with a bone. The machinery of overthinking kicks in and goes into overdrive, causing anxiety, distress, stomach aches and even panic attacks. Overthinkers grasp on to all sorts of ideas, then water them and feed them until their whole consciousness is suffocated by them.

The same process occurs with depressive thoughts like, 'No one really takes me seriously,' 'If I go to the party, no one will talk to me,' or 'My kids hate me, my partner does not like me, I am a total waste of space.' These thoughts occur alongside hundreds of other thoughts like, 'Are there aliens out there?', 'Will someone win the Lotto this week?' or 'That is an interesting fabric for a curtain.'

Since negative thoughts revolve around the concept of 'I, me or mine', the brain grasps these thoughts and spins them. Sometimes, holding on to these thoughts can lead to a depressive disorder, and the psychological treatment for it involves loosening the grasping on to these illogical ideas.

Many of our thoughts, including anxious and depressive ones, are the random musings of a busy brain. Our brain has evolved to notice our surroundings, constantly look for threats and come up with all sorts of ideas, the majority of which are idiotic, while some are sublime.

Thoughts are like bubbles that are often empty, valueless, quickly noticed and best let go. But many of us grasp on to them because they are our thoughts, therefore they must be important!

Viewing thoughts as *only* thoughts that don't necessarily need to be believed is radical.

Another example of grasping, of which I am guilty, is mentally owning mall car parks. After driving for what seems like forever, I find the perfect car park. It is under cover and not too far from the mall entrance. However, it is not so close that wayward supermarket trolleys might ding my car. I excitedly signal to take possession when another car, smaller and zippier than mine, steals it from the other direction.

She stole 'my' park. That park had my name on it. I saw it first. How dare she rob me of 'my' perfect space.

Hang on, was it really my park? Did it have my name on it? Did I really see it first? Because my mind already owned the park, I got angry and rageful when someone took it.

The same thing happens on the motorway. I'm driving along happily listening to Bach's Cello Suites when another car cuts me off without indicating. In my self-important mind, I believe that the asphalt in front of my car is mine and mine alone, so I get furious that someone has taken it without my explicit permission.

Our mind likes to own things – *my* car park, *my* road, *my* ideas, *my* house, *my* children, *my* family, *my* religion. We grasp on to this idea when we really do not own any of those things. If we really and truly owned them, we would have full control over them. At best, we are custodians of material things that exist totally independent of our control. We have a delusion that we own our children and our partner, but with that belief comes a lot of grief and suffering for all parties.

Instead of grasping to material things, ideas and people, let us hold them lightly in our hand, or better yet, learn how to let go. We do not own any of them. They are fleeting and impermanent. As Joseph Goldstein, an American Buddhist and meditation teacher advises, if we grasp too tightly, we get rope burn.

Grasping causes stress, suffering and dissatisfaction. The alternative is learning how to hold things lightly, which results in peace, contentment and happiness. The question now is how do we ungrasp?

CHAPTER 2

We are all crazy

I would like to think that, as a representative member of an intelligent species, I am rational. I try to be rational and logical but, for the most part, I am highly influenced by my emotions and cognitive limitations.

An example of my lack of rationality was when I enrolled in the zoology programme at university, which was a stepping stone to medical school. I enjoyed zoology but part of me wondered if I was suited to do something other than medicine.

I sat a very tiring psychological assessment to see what profession would suit me based on my personality and thinking style. The counsellor informed me that I was suited most to psychology or foreign relations and diplomacy. She cautioned that biological and physical science were not high on my list. Did I listen to her? Of course not. I was emotionally attached to becoming a doctor. It appealed to my heart, not my brain. My emotions overcame logic and reasoning.

Later in my medical training, I gravitated towards psychiatry, which is very close to psychology. Now, as a doctor of more than 30 years standing, I still wonder if working in foreign relations, the arts or even religious studies might have suited me better.

We have all been there. How many of us have found ourselves in a relationship with someone people had warned us against? Then, in the aftermath of a tumultuous separation, come to the realisation that the rational voices of our friends and relatives were indeed accurate.

If we genuinely believe that we are entirely rational beings, we are unquestionably deluding ourselves and embracing irrationality. The human mind possesses numerous smart operating features that aid our survival, but, simultaneously, they can subject us to immense stress and suffering.

The teachings of the Buddha emphasise the importance of recognising these characteristics of the mind and acquiring skills to effectively navigate and work with them.

· ·

Hack 5: Watch how the mind creates an endless list of desires.

· ·

Our minds are so good at convincing us that if only we had that hoodie/dress/pair of sunglasses then we would look cool. Same with wanting to go out with a certain girl or boy. You will only be happy if you marry that person. If we are that good at estimating our future happiness, our divorce rates would not be 50 per cent!

We have a built-in capacity to desire all sorts of things: objects, food, people, jobs, experiences and positions in society, alcohol, drugs, the latest jeans, the newest smart phone and the next exciting holiday.

The last thing I want you to think is that to desire and to crave is bad. In fact, to desire and crave is perfectly normal for humans. If we did not desire or crave, our species would have died out thousands of years ago.

From the Buddha's teachings, there are two kinds of desires. 'Chanda', which is wholesome and practical desire, and 'tanha', which is unwholesome and craving desire. Examples of chanda are the desire to help or the desire to have a peaceful and clear mind. Examples of tanha are an excessive desire for pleasure or possessions, or a desire to harm others.

For us to stay alive daily, we need food, water, a safe place to live and companionship. If we do not have any desire to eat or drink, we will not survive.

If I am someone who is satisfied with just a glass of water and a piece of bread daily, I will eventually become malnourished and dehydrated, which will result in my death.

If I am a farmer who is ecstatic and perfectly happy with a harvest of five apples for the season, my family and I will not survive.

We have a built-in desire-and-crave mechanism in our brain in order to survive. For most humans, this circuit has evolved so they are not easily satisfied. Satisfaction is brief, then we desire for more.

I love food. I organise most of my social catch-ups and networking over food. My family and many of my Asian friends are the same. We get excited planning which cuisine we will have or what restaurant we are going to visit. A lot of planning and menu checking occurs, which further fuels the craving. After a tummy-busting eating session, we'll force some dessert in to make sure we had a complete meal. We feel over-full and, for a moment, we appreciate the food, but before we even pay the bill, we are already planning our next meal … or worse, we'll be planning it while we're still enjoying our current meal!

I have a few friends who seem to have an insatiable desire to possess expensive shoes. One of my dear friends has a closet packed with designer shoes, some of which have never even seen daylight. Despite having a personal department store of shoes at home, they continue to get excited checking out the latest fashion releases. Most of their shoes cost thousands of dollars but cost is not an issue if the desire turns into craving.

Another good friend, a techie, is obsessed with the latest smart phones on the market. He upgrades his phone at least once a year and will queue for hours to acquire the latest model. Another friend, a mountain biker, upgrades his bike frequently, with some of his bikes costing more than $10,000 each. There is something within us that just does not get satisfied even if what we have is already good.

From a Buddhist perspective, attempting to fulfil all our desires will not lead to permanent happiness. Brief and temporary happiness perhaps, but the cycle of constant desire will not stop unless one cultivates wisdom, inner peace and contentment. The rational aspect of our mind can understand this, but the emotional part will rebel with the thought of controlling our desires.

Self-reflection

Was there ever a time when many of your desires were fulfilled?

Did you stop desiring after that?

Did the good feelings dissipate, only to be replaced by other desires?

Try to fulfil your desires for today. Pamper yourself with the best meal possible. Hang out with your best friends. Buy yourself that thing (please do not break the bank) you think will make you feel happy. At the end of the day, ask yourself if your desires have been totally extinguished.

When following the Buddha's teachings, it is important not to believe blindly. Experience the teachings yourself and see if what he says is true or not.

The Buddha's teachings on happiness and desire are upheld in psychology studies. When humans are presented with a positive stimulus, say winning the lottery or acquiring a new piece of jewellery or a new car, there is a temporary boost in happiness. Neurotransmitters, including dopamine, have been implicated in this spike of happiness.

However, with time, the levels of happiness go back to baseline. Unfortunately, this also happens with new relationships. There is a honeymoon phase, which is followed by a less exciting, hopefully more stable level of happiness. In psychology, this process of getting used to positive events, with the initial excitement and pleasure tailing off, is called habituation. We get used to things even if we thought that thing would really make us happy.

I habituated to money. I was a poor medical student in Manila, totally dependent on my family for everything – food, clothes, tuition and pocket money. I thought that I would be very happy once I was earning $3000 a month as a first-year training doctor in the US (this was in the early 1990s). From having nothing in my bank account to having thousands of dollars was hard to imagine.

Then as a first-year intern in New York, earning $3000 a month, I dreamed of becoming a consultant psychiatrist earning much more than that! Once I became a consultant psychiatrist, earning more than I needed, I still wanted a bit more, so I started working in private practice and doing extra jobs on the side.

Even now, having paid off my mortgage and earning way more than I can spend, I still occasionally buy a Lotto ticket just in case I win $20,000,000, which would mean I could buy that beachfront property in our neighbourhood …

The bottom line is that all of us must be careful with desires. Remember that we are highly powered desire-churning factories, and after quenching the desire, the happiness is short lived. Be careful of blindly following your desires thinking it will lead to long-term happiness. Often, it will not and the process of fulfilling those desires can have severe repercussions.

Hack 6: Desire and craving overpromise but underdeliver.

I know many married and committed people who blindly followed their desire to be with someone else who they found exciting or who they thought had the 'X factor', thereby forgoing a stable, predictable and possibly unexciting relationship. Most have ruined their relationships and left their families because they met 'the one'. Later, 'the one' turned out to be the worst nightmare of their lives. Of course, there has been the odd one who seemed to have made the right choice in a new partner, but these relationships appear to me as exceptions to the usual unhappy narrative.

As an amateur ocean swimmer, I marvel at how many of my swim mates have high-tech watches that track not just their swimming, but also running, cycling, walking, heart rate, sleep and even blood pressure. Though I have resisted getting such a watch for many years, I secretly pined for one. I thought that if I had one, my swimming pace would improve, I would swim more and I would look cool. To my surprise, my partner gifted me such a watch. I chose the basic model as I thought that it would be perfect for me: not too fancy or complicated, and the price was reasonable. Only after a few weeks of dutifully recording my swims, I noticed that the watch occasionally missed some of the laps I swam. Its recording of my sleep was not accurate. Then I got bored with the grey colour and hoped to get a more colourful strap. The perfect watch was now just another object that needed replacing soon!

Strong craving promised more than what it actually delivered. But when in the moment of intense desire, the brain promises us heaven and earth.

In addition to desire overpromising, it can also cause tension. We all have desires. Craving or grasping is a strong or more intense form of desire. We feel tense when we crave or grasp.

Here's an example. I am at a Buddhist temple for a five-day stay. One of the rules here is that we do not eat after midday. It is now after four o'clock on a humid summer afternoon. I desire ice cream, but it does not exist in this temple. Thinking about ice cream does not cause me distress. I am chilled about it because I am happy to follow the rules.

However, if my desire for ice cream becomes more intense, and I fantasise about crossing the street and ducking into the nearest convenience store for a salted caramel ice cream cone, my desire has shifted to craving and grasping – I *must* have *my* ice cream.

From just thinking about and desiring ice cream, I now crave ice cream. I am grasping the idea that I *want* ice cream. With the craving comes tension. I start getting angry at the stupid rules of Buddhist temples. I feel that I shouldn't have come here in the first place. I decide that a holiday at the beach would have been much nicer. I suffer.

∴∴∴∴∴∴∴∴∴∴∴∴∴∴∴∴∴∴∴∴∴∴∴∴∴∴∴∴∴

Hack 7: Stress is craving for things to be other than what they are.

∴∴∴∴∴∴∴∴∴∴∴∴∴∴∴∴∴∴∴∴∴∴∴∴∴∴∴∴∴

There is distinction between a simple desire and craving things to be different. Unlike a craving, a simple desire can be held lightly and not obsessively.

As a student, you might wish that your grades were higher or that you had less pimples, but overall, you are at peace with where you are at. There is minimal stress there. However, once you cross the desire bridge to the shores of craving, you begin to think that you *should* get higher grades and you *should not* have pimples. As a result, you feel tense and as if there is no peace. Instead, you have a strong compulsion to want things to be different.

I see many patients with chronic pain who also have poor sleep. I can divide them into two separate groups. One group believe that their chronic pain and poor sleep should be 100 per cent eliminated. They hate their pain and insomnia and believe their life is ruined because of them. They have obsessed about their symptoms to the point that their whole life revolves around wanting their situation to be totally different.

The second group has the same type of chronic pain and poor sleep, but they peacefully accept that they have symptoms, and they hope that things can improve. They desire change but have learned to live with their symptoms. They know that, as their doctor, I can only offer so much to alleviate their difficulties and that nothing is guaranteed to work. They desire some improvement but are not obsessed with or demanding change. They are not craving, they are not stressed and they are at peace.

Hack 8: Stress = $\frac{\text{Expectation}}{\text{Reality}}$

If we had totally rational minds, we would be very good at predicting future outcomes. The truth is we are often bad at managing our expectations, which then causes a lot of stress and suffering.

Jackie

For 20 years, I was involved in teaching at medical school. One of my responsibilities was to organise and supervise the final-year medical students' examinations in psychiatry. The psychiatry examination is daunting as it involves interviewing a 'patient' while being watched by two examiners. Actors play the role of patients presenting with various psychiatric symptoms, like depression, anxiety, psychosis, anger and even uncontrollable mania. The students interview the patient for 15 minutes, then the patient leaves while the student is interrogated by two senior doctors. Students prepare for many weeks, practising with each other and with their teachers.

One Friday afternoon while the examination was going on, I heard a loud knock on the door of my office, which was just outside the examination room. At the door was Jackie. She was crying hysterically; her whole body was shaking and her words were barely audible.

I ran through various possible scenarios. She'd studied hard and the examiners had failed her ... The actors had made it hard for her to pass ... Someone close to her had died ... I asked her what was going on.

After a few more minutes of inconsolable sobbing, she managed to utter, 'I didn't get a distinction in the exam, I only got a pass.'

I was speechless. The majority of students will celebrate a pass, but not Jackie. From grief, she became angry, complaining about the examination process and saying how unfair it was for students like her who'd prepared well and were on their way to getting distinction in all their subjects that year.

I felt attacked, as I had been running the examination process for many years. Telling her that she should be grateful for a pass didn't work. She *expected* a distinction.

It is easy to judge Jackie as an entitled medical student and feel that she is different from all of us. We might even feel some sense of schadenfreude, that she deserved a corrective experience for her inflated sense of entitlement. However, most, if not all of us, have harboured mini Jackies. All of us have had expectations, which when unfulfilled, have caused us grief.

41

Mrs Kennedy

I had a 55-year-old patient, Mrs Kennedy, who was distraught because her husband had been diagnosed with advanced melanoma that had spread to his brain, lungs and liver. She was told by his cancer specialist that he only had a few months to live and that the family should prepare for his passing.

In our consultation, she lashed out against the medical community for not having diagnosed her husband earlier in the course of his illness. She railed against the lack of effectiveness of the new chemotherapy drugs her husband had received. She was angry at God for allowing her husband to develop cancer, and not just any cancer, but a nasty melanoma.

'It is totally unfair! We are good Christians! We go to church weekly, we follow the Commandments, we give big donations – and this is what we get!'

Through my own sufferings and periods of self-reflection, I have developed an equation that states that stress equals expectation over reality. The more we expect and the further the desired results are from reality, the greater the suffering we experience.

Ajahn Brahm, a Buddhist monk and teacher in Perth, Australia, says, 'The more we expect, the more we get disappointed, the more suffering we have.' His teacher, Ajahn Chah, always reminded his monks, 'Mai nae,' or 'Maybe yes, maybe no,' as everything is uncertain. *Everything.* This includes the weather, our health, our relationships, our thoughts, our emotions, right down to sub-atomic particles. Everything is unstable and constantly changing.

Will your football team win this season? They have been playing well and the coach is excellent. 'Maybe yes, maybe no.'

Will you arrive at the airport on time? 'Maybe yes, maybe no.'

Will your partner be at home with a nice meal prepared and ready to welcome you with open arms? 'Maybe yes, maybe no.'

'Maybe yes, maybe no' reminds us that nothing is definite, which might sound pessimistic, but that is the reality of life.

We want certainty that our kids will grow up healthy and become happy adults. We want the government to deliver good healthcare and protect us from foreign invaders. We want the sun to always shine. We expect that after marrying 'the one', we will live happily ever after. 'Maybe yes, maybe no.'

If we examine the statement 'nothing is definite' with an unemotional and rational mind, we are bound to see that there are countless variables that determine a desired outcome or an expectation. It is impossible for anyone to control thousands or even millions of variables in any given equation in order to produce the desired result.

Jackie prepared extremely well for the examination and expected to get a distinction, as she'd been getting it in all her other subjects that year. She had all the necessary knowledge and skill to do well in her examination. However, she did not consider the fact that there are variables she did not have control over. The 'patient' might have had a bad day and been extra grumpy during the examination. The examiners might not have liked Jackie's thorough but very clinical and detached approach to the patient.

The reality of live examinations like this is that we can try to control the various components of the examination, for example medical knowledge and clinical interview techniques, but there will always be surprises.

I teach medical students about to take these examinations that a more realistic expectation is to study and aim for a distinction, but realistically and statistically, to expect they will only get a pass and, despite their best efforts, some will fail.

Mrs Kennedy had an unrealistic expectation that, given her strong faith and having lived an honourable life, God would spare her family from the ravages of illness.

Jackie and Mrs Kennedy both had unfulfilled expectations. Using the formula 'stress=expectation/reality', they both suffered, as their desired outcomes were far from what occurred.

The Buddha taught that suffering often arises from craving or grasping. Jackie clung to the concept that she was a medical student who deserved a distinction. She was wedded to the identity that she would gain a distinction for all her subjects. Mrs Kennedy clung to the idea that by being a good Christian, God would spare her and her family from horrible illnesses. Grasping to expectations of how things should be caused suffering for them both.

Does that mean we abandon having goals or aspirations? Since we cannot control all the variables in our lives, should we just sit back, relax and let nature take its course, wherever it would bring us? That is lacking in wisdom. Instead, we can have goals, aspirations and targets as long as we do not grasp on to them.

We can work hard and pour our resources towards an outcome, but we must realise that anything can happen, as we do not have full control of all the variables. We can never be sure of the outcome – 'maybe yes, maybe no' – as anything is possible.

Instead of clinging to an outcome, or how things should be in the future, an attitude of openness is healthier and more realistic. Jackie would not have crumbled if her approach had been to study as best as she could while being open to whatever result she received. Mrs Kennedy would not have been as distraught and angry if she had been accepting of the nature of being born as a human. Humans are born, humans get sick and humans die, regardless of whether they have faith to a supreme being or not.

· ·

Hack 9: Train your mind to acknowledge that your reality is just one of eight billion other realities.

· ·

Without being dramatic, I occasionally tell people that we are all a bit psychiatrically unwell in this world. We rely on our sensory organs to deliver input into our brains from which we make conclusions about our experiences. The problem is our sensory organs are not the most accurate and the quality is variable. Things we see are not always what they seem.

Self-reflection

How many times while watching a game of sport have you energetically disagreed with others whether a goal/try/point was valid or not?

How many times have you watched the video playback and reluctantly conceded that you were wrong?

How many times have you thought you heard something only to find that it was not what you thought?

How many times have you tasted, touched or smelled things only to find they were not what you thought?

Despite not being a cognitive neuroscientist, the Buddha made this profound statement: 'The eye, the ear, the nose, the tongue, the body, the mind – this is the way through which one is a perceiver of the world and a conceiver of the world.'

He is saying that the way we see 'reality' is a by-product not just of our senses, but also of our past conditioning, our biases, our prejudices and our mental state. The world we see is highly subjective and synthesised by the brain.

This insight by the Buddha predated the cognitive neuroscience concept of predictive processing by 2600 years. Predictive processing suggests that our perception of reality is not solely based on sensory inputs but also on the perceiver's knowledge, past experiences and associations.

What we see as reality is based on very subjective grounds. The world we see and experience is a product of our own minds. I am not saying that the world out there is a fiction of imagination. The world and the universe exist, but how we view them is our own subjective experience.

In the US, it is so common to be offered grapefruit juice for breakfast and people look at me quizzically when I say I cannot drink it because it is bitter. A few people have joked that I must be teasing them because grapefruit juice is sweet and delicious. It turns out that three of my sisters also find grapefruit juice bitter, so it's not all in my head. Further geeky research into this showed that we might be supertasters, and our taste sensitivity to bitterness is different from other people's.

The sources of information – our senses – are highly variable and always limited. Then, we expect the brain, which has its own bugs, to synthesise all the information to create a representation of our experience.

What kind of bugs do we have in our wiring? As well as an overzealous desire system and unrealistic expectations, the brain has built-in cognitive biases or distorted ways of interpreting events. The brain also creates stories or dialogues that are highly influenced by past events or even genes. Our memories are also faulty and sometimes we even create false memories.

Using a highly variable input system and a faulty computer, we make conclusions about everything in the world.

Mr J

I was on call as a resident physician in psychiatry at the Philadelphia Veterans Administration Hospital. It was a quiet evening with just a handful of patients in the emergency room. The outgoing resident physician had warned me to watch out for Mr J, the patient in bed three. Mr J was a veteran who had severe post-traumatic stress disorder from his experiences during the Vietnam War. The outgoing doctor had told me to be careful, as Mr J had become violent towards Asian staff members.

As a Chinese-looking Filipino, I got a bit anxious. I was a hobbit compared to Mr J, who was a hulking six-foot-six piece of solid muscle. I stayed away from his bed as much as possible, but when his IV line came out and we needed to give him medications, the nurse was nowhere to be found. I had to insert his IV line, so I informed other staff to call security if I got into trouble.

Mr J was fast asleep when I slowly approached his bed. From a distance, I called out, 'Mister J, Mister J, I am Doctor Fernando and I need to put in your IV.' No response.

I got closer and closer, and my heart got faster and faster. He did not answer. Finally, I got close to his bed and tapped the end of it in a feeble attempt to wake him up. He suddenly jumped up, sat on the bed and stared at me.

I introduced myself with the softest voice possible. 'I am Doctor Fernando and I need to check your IV line, if that is okay with you?'

In the warmest and friendliest bass-baritone voice, he said, 'That's okay, Doctor Fernando, go ahead.'

After I successfully inserted his line, we got talking. He'd had a horrific experience in Vietnam, where he had been tortured. As a result, every time he smelled Asian spices, he had a surge of anxiety. When he saw Asian people, he had panic attacks. Before he got treatment for PTSD, he had assaulted Asian-looking men amid unprovoked rage attacks.

Mr J's sense of perception is different from most of ours. The Asian spices that trigger memories of home for me induce anxiety for Mr J. The visual cue of an Asian person activates a threat response in him. Following his trauma, his view and experience of the world was different from yours or mine. To tell him that he is wrong is erroneous. For him, his interpretation of the world makes sense. It aims to protect him.

All of us are like Mr J. We have our own experience of the world. From this, we create our own stories and dialogues, many of which are unhelpful and cause us stress and anxiety.

Not believing all our thoughts and scripts in our heads as true can be a relief for many people. I see many people in my clinic who, despite their accomplishments professionally, in society and as parents, view themselves as 'losers', as not good enough and as constantly needing to do more. Many people have unending dialogues in their head that people are out to get them or that they are not worthy of praise or happiness.

All of us have prejudiced or biased interpretations of the world inside our heads. No one is perfectly rational and sane. Our thoughts, emotions, beliefs and philosophies are creations of our limited senses and buggy minds. If we accept that all of us are unwell because of our faulty minds, then one implication is that we need to be more compassionate towards everyone.

Ajahn Amaro, one of my teachers in the Thai Forest Tradition, said, 'If we consider that we are sharing a psychiatric ward with our fellow inmates, then we will be a lot more forgiving of each other.

'We need to create space in our heart for all the different versions of the world, for others' version of reality.'

Does that mean we should allow crazy and unskilful behaviours to go unchecked? Unskilful behaviours are actions that result in harm to oneself or others.

The Buddha, in his incredible wisdom, wants us to be understanding and compassionate towards others who we perceive as different. But at the same time, he knows that we all must live together harmoniously so he gave specific suggestions on how we can do that. It's not all about being tolerant of each other. We must behave a certain way to promote peace.

Hack 10: Catch yourself when you are in a papañca.

One psychological process that most of us engage in without knowing is papañca. This word comes from the original language of Buddha's written teachings – Pali – and is the word the Buddha used to describe the process of mental proliferation when the mind becomes caught in a spin of thoughts, stories and ideas. This is also known as being 'lost in thought'. Sometimes, the mind swirls narratives with such strength that they feel solid, permanent and true. At full force, they can spin like tornadoes in our heads.

Carla and Joe

Carla never saw eye to eye with her in-laws. Coming from a working-class family, she had always felt that Joe's parents, who were successful business owners, looked down on her.

Joe and Carla were celebrating their wedding anniversary with a meal Joe had cooked. Carla was feeling blessed that Joe was such a loving and caring husband when she got a text from Joe's mother inviting them to attend a party at Joe's parents' house. The moment Carla read the text message, her mind went into overdrive, a papañca.

She started thinking about how hypocritical it was of Joe's mother to invite her when she never felt welcomed by the family. She thought of one incident when Joe's mother hadn't mentioned the expensive dress she had worn to a party, which she saw as proof that her mother-in-law thought she had poor taste in clothes. She then wondered why she ever married Joe, when she would have been better off marrying Patrick, a bus driver, who was in the same social class as her. If she'd married Patrick, she would have been happier, and her in-laws would not be haughty and hateful. She remembered an argument about finances she'd had with Joe a few weeks earlier and saw it as proof that their relationship was doomed. She started to wonder whether she should get out of the relationship, as it would never work out. She started sobbing, and all the while Joe had no idea what was going on.

This mental tornado, triggered by Carla's mother-in-law's text, went on for a few minutes. Prior to receiving the text, she had been happy and content in her relationship and thankful for having such a loving husband. Two minutes after the text, she was already thinking of divorce.

It turned out that Joe's mother had organised a party to celebrate Joe and Carla's wedding anniversary. At the party, Joe's parents thanked Carla for making their son a much happier man.

All of us tend to get into a papañca from time to time. When sensitive topics are brought up, for example, the rising crime rates and crumbling infrastructure in New Zealand, me and my friends go into a papañca. One group will go on an emotive litany of how the current government is a total failure. Others will blame immigrants, while some will spew vitriol against previous governments that did not do their job properly. This can result in heated discussions and frayed relationships that never get resolved.

Papañca can be triggered by emotive stimuli like politics and religion. However, it can be brought on by any neutral sensory input, like sight, sound, touch, taste, smell or random memories.

Mr J, my Vietnam vet patient, went into a hurricane-level papañca when he smelled Asian spices.

Seeing someone who looks like someone we love (or hate) can trigger narratives and stories that send us into some dream-like state.

The Buddha was clear about papañca. 'Papañca should be known, one should regard it as a disease, and one should seek cessation from it.'

He said that being entangled in papañca is suffering.

I still engage in papañca but after following many of the Buddha's hacks for an easier life, I am able to catch myself when I am in one. I tell myself, 'You are papañca-ing again!' Then I smile. Papañca loses its energy.

We are all crazy. We have uncontrollable desires. We are not good at managing expectations. We are rubbish at perceiving the world around us accurately, and we have tornadoes in our heads that cause stress and suffering.

The Buddha, however, believed that we can wake up from our ignorant state. He instructed his students to undergo a multi-pronged educational programme aimed at experiencing less stress and more peace. His programme was threefold.

1. We need to develop wisdom and become familiar with our crazy minds.
2. Since we are social creatures and live with other people, we must make sure we do not cause harm to others.
3. There are several practices that will lead to knowing more about the mind, living peacefully and managing stress and suffering.

As we now know how crazy we all are, the next chapters will cover how we can uncrazy ourselves, live kindly and wake ourselves from our sleep-walking state.

CHAPTER 3

Living harmlessly

In the past two decades, I have read countless self-help books in my quest to find helpful, evidence-based techniques for how to be happy and how to suffer less. A common denominator in these books has been the focus on 'self' – for example, self-esteem and self-improvement. Very rarely do they put any emphasis on being kind or, at the very least, not causing harm to others. One theory for this is that telling people to behave kindly might make them feel bad about themselves. This is the opposite of what the self-help movement is trying to achieve, which is to make people feel good.

From a Buddhist perspective, not causing harm to the self and others, in other words living ethically, is the foundation for achieving genuine and lasting happiness. Practising harmlessness is even considered more important than learning meditation.

When I visited Burma for the first time in 2016, I was excited to talk to the monks I met about their personal experiences regarding their Buddhist education and training. I was surprised that many of the teenage novices or junior monks were not routinely taught meditation. One 14-year-old novice told me that he meditated for just a few minutes a day. I had expected that he would have been meditating for hours day and night.

In fact, he was an outlier because most novices do not meditate at all. Instead, they spend hours each day learning about the Buddhist scriptures.

This confused me as I thought mindfulness meditation was essential in any Buddhist training. I asked senior monks why the junior monks were not taught how to meditate. They said that in the formative years, as well as learning the Buddhist scriptures, the emphasis was on practising harmlessness or ethical living. The aim of Buddhist training, which is enlightenment and unconditional peace, will not be achieved if harmlessness or ethical living is not practised.

A few years after my visit to Burma, I was at a conference in San Diego where the topic was the practice and research of contemplative sciences. The majority of the attendees were meditation practitioners, monks and nuns – Buddhist, Hindu and Christian – psychologists, therapists, researchers and neuroscientists. There was a vigorous debate on the pros and cons of teaching the US armed forces mindfulness meditation without teaching harmlessness or ethics.

On one hand, teaching mindfulness to soldiers might prevent depression, post-traumatic stress disorder and suicide. Mindfulness becomes a mental armour or mind shield for soldiers when they are actively deployed and exposed to war. On the other hand, teaching mindfulness without ethics will produce efficient, concentrated and mindful killing machines, as these soldiers have been taught to use mindfulness of the breath while aiming and shooting their weapons.

The debate on whether mindfulness should be taught with or without the concept of harmlessness continues to this day. The majority of the secular mindfulness courses, whether online, in apps or in person, omit teachings of harmlessness or ethical living, and my view on the matter has changed over the years.

In the beginning, I felt that teaching mindfulness without harmlessness was better than not teaching mindfulness at all. Also, there is some research evidence that shows practising mindfulness can lead to compassionate actions.

However, after a couple of decades of trying to practise mind techniques taught by the Buddha, I now understand why the learning and practising of harmlessness is essential to our search for genuine happiness. I also understand why living kindly without causing harm is the cornerstone of training for the followers of the Buddha. Mindfulness without kindness is superficial and incomplete.

What is harmlessness?

Harmlessness involves behaving in a manner that does not cause violence, injury, or damage to other beings – both humans and animals. It is a way of relating to others out of kindness and compassion, versus acting out of greed, selfishness, ignorance or anger. To act ethically comes from a heart that understands that all of us want to be happy, to be at peace and to be free from suffering, pain and anxiety.

Why should we behave ethically? How is this related to our goal of genuine happiness? Aren't the majority of the wealthiest and most powerful people on Earth behaving unethically?

Unlike other religions, in Buddhism, the compulsion to act kindly, ethically and harmlessly does not come as a commandment from a higher being. It is not a mandate from God or a prophet. If we do not act harmlessly, we will not be damned to some sort of everlasting torment. Instead, the Buddha gave guidelines for living ethically for two practical reasons, both of which will assist us in our quest to be happy.

First, the Buddha understood that as social creatures, humans live with other humans. Second, the Buddha knew that when people act kindly, with generosity and compassion, our brains will reward us by making us feel good.

As social creatures, we do not live in a vacuum. Most of us live and interact with other humans. Almost everywhere we go, we interact with other humans – even if some of us don't much enjoy it.

A friend of mine, an Austrian scientist, enjoys being alone, as he finds most human interactions tedious and stressful. He excitedly told me that he was going to spend a few weeks alone on the Svalbard Islands in the Arctic Circle. This would be heaven for him as he'd be able to disconnect from other humans. Unfortunately, this was not to be, as his Norwegian guide made sure to check in on him several times during his stay just to make sure he hadn't frozen to death.

Some people have a mistaken notion that they can avoid other humans when they live in Buddhist monasteries. Though some monasteries limit verbal communication, practising what's called 'noble silence', monks and nuns still need to try to live harmoniously with each other if what they want to achieve is peace and happiness.

Since we live with other humans, we inevitably impact them and they impact us. The quality of our interactions and relationships will affect both their happiness and our own.

When we harm others through our speech or actions, there is high likelihood that this will lead others to cause harm to us. Triggered by our harmful behaviour, other people's actions can result in our unhappiness, torment and suffering – the total opposite of our goal of being genuinely happy.

Almost always, the impact of harsh language or unkind action is immediate, but sometimes it can be delayed. On a Buddhist timeline, it might even occur many lifetimes afterwards.

If we treat the people we live, work and interact with the way we ourselves would like to be treated, they will generally treat us with kindness as well. Even animals know this. When they are treated well, when they are fed and made to feel safe, they become softer, less wild and might even want to live with us. Shout at them, throw stones at them, cause them harm and they will become hostile to us. Kindness and warm-heartedness beget kindness and warm-heartedness.

When we act kindly, in a harmless way, we offer other beings the priceless gift of safety. Our kind actions make others feel safe. They know that they will be accepted, treated warmly and will not be harmed. They can relax and be themselves: spontaneous, free, happy and without concerns. Even without thinking about it, they will give us back the gift of safety too.

When we behave with goodness, generosity and kindness, our heart is delighted. We have the same feeling when we see others behave kindly and unselfishly towards other people or animals.

On the other hand, when we cause harm to others through violence, spreading lies or stealing, our conscience aches. Even without anyone telling us, a part of us is aware that we have done something wrong. The same thing occurs when we see others behave badly, unkindly or harshly towards others. Our heart aches and feels some type of pain.

The Buddha described two mind qualities that serve as humans' natural internal moral compass, Hiri and Ottappa. Hiri is our internal moral compass and self-respect, while Ottapa is respect for others. Hiri and Ottappa are our inborn shame and fear when we commit unwholesome actions.

Our inborn ability to have this moral sensitivity and respect for others is probably genetically coded, and therefore unrelated to religion or philosophical belief. This internal discomfort is present in most people, irrespective of their religious beliefs, except perhaps extreme sociopaths.

William

Early in my career as a psychiatrist, I saw William – a veteran in his seventies – for treatment for depression. He had been treated with various antidepressants, but his depression never went away. William agreed to become one of my first psychotherapy patients. He was an unusually tall man and was built like an ox. He had a sad face and his body seemed perpetually stooped. My windowless box of an office felt extra cramped during our weekly sessions.

For a few months, we explored his history in detail – his childhood years, his family life, his war experience, his anxieties, fears and concerns. His depression was not improving with therapy and, despite regular supervision sessions with my professor, I could not seem to make headway with his symptoms. I was becoming impatient and wanted to try him on a new medication.

Around the sixth month of therapy, William started the session by saying, 'Doctor Fernando, I need to be totally honest with you.'

My mind went into overdrive – a papañca! Was William about to tell me that I was hopeless as a doctor? Was he about to complain about his lack of progress? Had he become psychotic and homicidal towards me?

Without saying a word, I gave him space to continue. Softly and slowly, he said, 'I killed someone.'

My mind went blank, followed by a tornado-strength papañca of thoughts and worries. I had not trained for this. With one thump from his massive fist, I could become his next victim …

Then he proceeded to tell me his story. After his tour of duty, he came home to find his son had changed as a result of severe bullying by a classmate. He met with his son's teachers and school administration, with no resolution. He met with the family of the bully but the parents felt helpless about the situation.

Before graduating from high school, his son killed himself. A few years after his son's death, William carefully planned the perfect revenge. For months, he studied the bully's daily routines, then he killed the man in a neighbourhood where random killings occurred frequently.

That had been 10 years earlier, and he had never confessed the murder to anyone until our consultation. This huge man cried and sobbed for the rest of the session.

As a crime had been committed, I discussed the case with my employer and their lawyers. But since it was a confession of a past crime, and there was no suggestion that a future crime would be committed, I could not disclose anything to the police. I was strongly advised to continue with our therapy.

When he arrived for our next session, I barely recognised William. He was a different man. He stood with a straight back and looked taller than he had over the past six months. His face was calm and peaceful. He told me that for the first time in more than 15 years he felt light in himself. His depressive symptoms had mostly resolved. I carried on seeing him for a total of two years and he remained depression free.

I cannot be 100 per cent certain what led to the resolution of his depression. One theory is that, for more than a decade, he had carried the burden of knowing that he had deliberately taken the life of another human being. Even if he felt that his act was justified, a huge part of him knew that it was wrong. He was not a religious person and did not fear any spiritual or eternal repercussion for his action. However, deep inside he knew he had caused terrible harm and he'd needed to unburden himself to someone.

Precepts from the Buddha

The Buddha is clear that we must act harmlessly to ourselves and to others in our search for lasting happiness. In the Dhammapada, one of the most read texts of the Buddha's teachings, he summarised all his 45 years of teachings in 10 words: 'Refrain from unwholesome actions, perform good actions, purify the mind.'

As living in a harmless way was one of the Buddha's most important teachings, he did not let his audience speculate as to what was wholesome and what was not. Instead, he gave clear directions on which actions to take and which to avoid. He strongly suggested – but didn't command – a set of guidelines for living harmlessly, which are called the precepts.

Different Buddhist traditions have varying numbers of precepts. Some Buddhist traditions have five, while monks of the Theravadan school follow 227. Here, I will focus on the five precepts that many students of the Buddha's teachings try to follow:

1. kind and honest speech
2. harmlessness
3. non-stealing
4. avoiding sexual misconduct
5. avoiding intoxicants.

Ajahn Sucitto is clear about why we need to follow the precepts. 'I don't do to you what I don't want you to do to me. I don't steal things and I don't lie to you because I know I wouldn't want those things to happen to me. And I don't sexually abuse or violate others, and so forth. I have that sense of respect for other beings. So that's for my welfare, for the welfare of others and leads to peace.'

We do not need any prophet, teacher or God to command us how to behave if we truly know the power of our words and actions. These precepts are not commandments. They are not absolute rules. They are guidelines, which if followed as well as possible, often result in a peaceful mind and an unburdened heart.

Lay Buddhists in the Theravadan tradition regularly ask monks or nuns for the opportunity to follow the precepts. They are not commanded to follow the precepts. Many will follow the precepts strictly for a day, while some will commit to doing it for their whole life. Other practitioners will recite the precepts every morning after their meditation practice. Asking to follow the precepts becomes a regular reminder of how to behave, as our actions impact on ourselves and everyone around us.

When we follow the precepts and avoid actions that cause harm to others, our minds are clear, rested and free from unnecessary worry. We know that we have acted kindly. We do not carry the burden of harmful acts. We do not fear backlash or consequences of harmful actions. When we try to follow the precepts, our relationships are more harmonious. If we want to build a solid foundation for our happiness, following the precepts makes sense.

Why bother with the precepts? Because our thoughts, words and actions impact others. If we accept that what we think, say and do affects others, we will behave a certain way to keep some peace.

If humans want to live together harmoniously, happily and with less suffering, following the precepts is a no-brainer. Can you imagine if all humans just followed the single rule of not harming others throughout their lives? We would live in a totally different world, one in which there would be no cheating, lying, stealing, murder, child abuse, elder abuse, animal abuse, genocide or war.

Humans are not that simple, and most of us will not follow rules all the time, as there are competing motivations. That is why in Buddhist communities there are regular reminders to follow the precepts because they are often forgotten, despite our best intentions.

· ·

Hack 11: If you want to be a better person, try practising the precepts.

· ·

From a Buddhist point of view, even when we live alone, following the precepts is beneficial as it cultivates good character, compassion, self-discipline and mindfulness. Kind and compassionate actions even when in solitude will influence our future experiences.

If you are living with another person, would you want to live with someone who is callous and insensitive? Someone who would thoughtlessly kill animals? Someone who has a potty mouth, who lies and talks behind your back? Someone who steals your food and clothes? Someone who is out of control and intoxicated? Someone whose sexual energy is uncontrollable and who brings random sexual partners into your space?

Or would you rather live with someone who follows the precepts? Someone who is sensitive, truthful, harmless, respectful of property, conscious of sensual boundaries and in control of their faculties? Someone who is just a decent human being? Someone who has clear thoughts, fragrant and meaningful words? Someone who makes you feel safe? Someone who is a better person? If you wouldn't want to live with someone like that in the first example, why would you want to *be* someone like that?

When we try to live harmlessly and ethically, mindful of our speech and behaviours, we tell every living being around us, 'I will not harm you.'

. . . .

Hack 12: Following the precepts is a practice of mindfulness.

. . . .

For me, being conscious of following the precepts most days has become an exercise of mindfulness. Even though I still have a long way to go, I have become more aware of the impact of my thoughts, the words that I say and how I behave. Ajahn Sucitto told me that practising the precepts is mindfulness of behaviour. And he is right; practising the precepts means paying mindful attention to our impulses, thoughts, speech and action.

The Zen master Thích Nhất Hạnh crafted the five mindfulness trainings, which are derived from the precepts. He viewed the precepts not as orders from the Buddha but as a framework to be mindful of our thinking, speech and actions. He believed that when we are more mindful of our speech and actions, we create more happiness for ourselves and the world around us. Here is a shortened version of the five mindfulness trainings.

1. Aware of the suffering caused by the destruction of life, I am committed to cultivating the insight of interbeing and compassion and learning ways to protect the lives of people, animals, plants and minerals.

2. Aware of the suffering caused by exploitation, social injustice, stealing and oppression, I am committed to practising generosity in my thinking, speaking and acting.

3. Aware of the suffering caused by sexual misconduct, I am committed to cultivating responsibility and learning ways to protect the safety and integrity of individuals, couples, families and society.

4. Aware of the suffering caused by unmindful speech and the inability to listen to others, I am committed to cultivating loving speech and compassionate listening in order to relieve suffering and to promote reconciliation and peace in myself and among other people, ethnic and religious groups and nations.

5. Aware of the suffering caused by unmindful consumption, I am committed to cultivating good health, both physical and mental, for myself, my family and my society by practising mindful eating, drinking and consuming.

CHAPTER 4

Precept one: kind and honest speech

In my work as a psychiatrist, patients often talk about the immense hurt they have experienced as a result of the actions of other people. More than unkind actions, my patients talk about the impact of hurtful words from parents, siblings, partners, children, relatives, teachers, co-workers and bosses.

Vicky

Vicky told me how, when they were kids, her brother Max repeatedly made comments that she was fat. Later, Vicky developed weight issues, which she successfully addressed by becoming a competitive triathlete. Now in her seventies, Vicky still feels hurt by the comments Max made many decades ago. Recently, she found the courage to confront Max about his hurtful comments. He was remorseful and asked for forgiveness. Though he couldn't remember making those comments, he admitted that when he was young, he'd had a tendency to be careless with words.

Unkind words are like darts that come out of our mouths. They can cause irreparable wounds and scar people for life, even if we

66

Precept one: kind and honest speech

did not mean them to. As social animals, we put tremendous value on being liked and accepted. Harmful words can make us feel disliked, rejected and unworthy. Meanwhile, kind words are reassuring and make us feel worthy and accepted.

Bhikkhu Bodhi, an American Buddhist monk and scholar, summed it up well, saying, 'Speech can break lives, create enemies and start wars, or it can give wisdom, heal divisions and create peace.'

When the Buddha listed 10 harmful actions that humans engaged in, four of them pertain to speech. They are:

1. lying
2. sowing discord
3. harsh speech
4. mindless chatter.

. . . .

Hack 13: Before you say anything, check whether it is true and timely, whether it will result in peace and whether it is gentle and not gossip.

. . . .

Krishnan Venkatesh, a Buddhist teacher, said, 'Mastering our minds begins with mastering our mouths.' We all talk a lot – apparently anywhere from 2000 to more than 5000 words a day. With that amount of words coming out, there are bound to be untruths or unkind words eventually, and our chance of causing harm is high.

When I've visited Buddhist monasteries, I've noticed that most monks and nuns are softly spoken and are measured in

67

their speech. In fact, many Buddhist monks and nuns practise noble silence, which sees them avoid unnecessary talking. They have no obligation to talk or to fill the silence with useless chatter. Noble silence reflects inner calm and peace.

When I first heard about the precept of kind and honest speech, I deluded myself into believing that I did not have issues with unkind speech. I thought that since I rarely deliberately lied, I was all good with that precept. That is until I checked the criteria laid down for kind speech. Only then did I realise that I had a lot of work to do on my speech.

The Buddha himself outlined the characteristics of kind speech. It should be true and timely. It should cause harmony and avoid discord. It should be gentle. It should be meaningful and it should not be gossip.

Looking at his criteria, I realised that I have not always been kind in my speech. I have said things at the wrong time. I have said things harshly and angrily. I have gossiped. Even if I had only been unkind in my speech once a week throughout my life, I would have said hurtful things at least 2900 times.

At a societal level, it seems that most of us are not practising kind speech. Given the power of the internet and social media, the impact of unkind and untruthful speech in causing disharmony and conflict is beyond imaginable.

Let us look at and reflect on the various characteristics of kind speech one at a time.

1. Is what you are about to say 100 per cent true?

If we are always truthful with our words, our family and friends feel safe with us. Nothing is concealed. They know us with our warts and all. We are seen as honest and someone who can be trusted. Our relationships are straightforward and have strong foundations. Life is simpler and easier as nothing needs to be covered up or concealed. We are an open book with no hidden agenda.

On the other hand, telling deliberate lies makes life complicated. The German philosopher Friedrich Nietzsche said, 'I'm not upset that you lied to me, I'm upset that from now on I can't believe you.'

If I tell a lie, for example, I make up a false story that my boss really likes me when in fact he can't stand me, I must come up with future lies to protect the first lie. If I come home looking stressed because my boss has scolded me again, I have to come up with another story to explain why I look stressed. I make up a story that a colleague is jealous because my boss prefers me … and so on.

Lies tend to self-proliferate to protect previous lies, and once we're locked in a string of falsehoods, escape becomes difficult. The endless lies cause stress and suffering. Eventually, the uncovering of the series of lies results in shame, embarrassment and mistrust. It would have been simpler if, from the beginning, we'd just been truthful.

Studies have shown that most of us are generally honest, with one study indicating that the majority of us tell zero to two lies per day. However, there is a minority of prolific liars, around 1 per cent of participants of a research study who lie an average of 15 times per day.

Lying should not be dismissed as simply bad or evil. The most common reason for lying is to protect oneself or others. Kids often lie to protect themselves from punishment or embarrassment, which is not necessarily a bad thing. People also lie to protect others from harm. Instead of quickly judging a person who lies as a wrongdoer or someone who deserves to be punished, understanding why a lie has been told will provide a clearer picture of the motivation behind it. Nevertheless, regardless of the reason or intention for lying, sticking with the truth, or sometimes not saying anything at all, makes life less complicated.

2. Is what you are about to say properly timed?

Words are powerful in that they can promote connection, and healing and express love and appreciation; unmindfully spoken words can cause the reverse. Even if what you say is true, poor timing can have horrific effects. Sometimes, words – even if truthful – are better not said at all.

The Connor family

At dinnertime, the mother of the Connor family, Lucy, asks her children how their day at school went. The three children, Theresa, William and David, give their nightly report in front of the whole family. During examination weeks, youngest son David dreads these nightly accounts. All the kids are smart and do well academically and in sports. However, while Theresa and William often top their classes and are straight-A students, David, who excels at sport, often gets Bs. When this happens, his mother zeroes in on him and tells him that Bs are not good enough. She constantly compares David to his other siblings.

Despite David's average grades, he was accepted into one of the country's top engineering schools. In his third year, he dropped out due to depression. In therapy, a recurrent theme that plagued David was his belief that he was not good enough. In his mind, he constantly played over those dinnertime comments his mother made in front of the whole family. His mother's comments humiliated him and made him feel small.

While it might have been factually correct that David wasn't as smart as his siblings, those comments were ill-timed. If his mother had talked to David about his marks in private, and offered helpful suggestions, he would not have been scarred so deeply.

Timing is critical for effective communication. When your partner is angry at you because you are late for a date again, responding by recounting your partner's mistakes will cause further chaos. Instead, accepting fault is smart, and talking about your partner's issues later is smarter.

When people want to solve conflict, for example, relationship difficulties or disagreements with workmates, timing is crucial. Conflict resolution should only be attempted when both parties are in a calm and open mental state.

Addressing your partner's spendthrift ways when she is upset about your drinking habits is poor timing. Informing a colleague at a company-wide meeting that his lunch stank out the office kitchen is bad timing. You might even earn an enemy for life.

However, timing one's speech is not always easy. When emotional and upset, there is a gut-level urgency that drives us to blurt out our thoughts. Timing our speech requires restraint and a certain degree of mindfulness. If practised regularly, timing our speech will benefit others in that it will make them feel safe around us. It also benefits us as we develop patience, a mental characteristic that is linked to happiness and peace.

3. Is what you are about to say going to result in peace and harmony?

Apart from trying to be truthful all the time, we need to ask ourselves what our intention is for saying something. Is it coming from a place of loving kindness or good will for others? Or are we saying things to put others down?

Remember Max, who constantly called his sister Vicky fat? It is true that Vicky was overweight, but his intention was to humiliate her and put her down. True speech is not necessarily kind speech. An old saying goes, 'The tongue is a boneless weapon trapped between the teeth.' When we are not careful with our speech, our words – even if they are true – can cause irreversible damage.

Rachel and Mark

Rachel was a very dedicated doctor who spent most of her life caring for patients dying from cancer. I developed a good friendship with Rachel as we shared a lot of similar interests in sports and philosophy.

One afternoon, along the hospital corridor, I bumped into Mark, a well-regarded scientist, who I aspired to be like in terms of research output. He invited me for coffee, which surprised me as we usually just said hello to each other in the halls of the hospital.

As soon as I got my coffee, he said that he'd seen Rachel and I hanging out. He then launched into a detailed story of how he and Rachel had been in a relationship for many years and that Rachel had cheated on him. He told me that I should be very careful of Rachel as she was a two-faced ... well, you can use your imagination here.

After that conversation with Mark, I noticed how my attitude towards Rachel changed. I became aloof and guarded and felt distrusting of her even though I had not heard her side of the story.

Not long after that I went on holiday and when I got back, Rachel had left the hospital and moved away. I never got to ask for her side of the story.

A few months later, a friend told me another version of what had happened between Rachel and Mark. They told me that Mark had physically assaulted Rachel after she had confronted him about his ongoing affair with another doctor.

I had always prided (or deluded) myself on being objective and giving people the benefit of the doubt. However, a few unkind words about Rachel from Mark saw my view of Rachel tainted. I was aware that Mark might not have been completely truthful, but his words impacted how I unconsciously related to Rachel.

Another form of unkind speech is malicious talk disguised as concern for others.

In recent political elections, the desire of voters to convince other people of their particular values, under a brittle veneer of education and enlightenment, has resulted in insults, vitriol and scorn being thrown around. This process of debate should reaffirm democracy, which is used to promote peace and harmony. However, this democratic process is misappropriated, and the ubiquity of social media has multiplied the impact of hurtful declarations, as hundreds if not thousands become witness to toxic exchanges between friends and families. Once private, healthy, verbal debates have become public spectacles of hateful speech on social media. People have 'unfriended' family and friends – both online and in real life – over politicians who do not really care for them. I advise people to avoid heated discussions on politics or religion as they often degenerate into personal attacks, which ruin relationships.

Before people engage in a discussion about a controversial topic, they need to ask themselves how open they are to listening to someone who has a different opinion. Will they be able to agree to disagree and remain friends? If the answer is no, then the discussion is not worth having.

I have made it a personal policy to avoid discussing contentious topics even with loved ones and lifelong friends if I know that my views or their views are set and unchangeable for now. It is not worth fracturing precious relationships over ideas or concepts that might change in the future anyway.

Having said that, I have occasionally engaged with divisive topics when I've been curious as to how other people view the world. I once took an Uber in Sydney and, when I saw that the driver's name was Muhammad, I greeted him with 'Salaam Alaikum,' which means 'Peace be upon you' in Arabic. He responded, 'Wa Alaikum Salaam,' which means 'And upon you be peace.'

He asked me where I was from and what I was doing in Sydney, then he went on tell me that he was from Afghanistan and had been in Sydney for more than 15 years. He cautioned me that where I lived, near Kings Cross, was 'dirty' because of the bars and sex workers. He went on to talk about how westerners had conquered many countries and imposed their culture on others. He said that he was trying to save money because he wanted to go back to Afghanistan, as he hated living in a western country. He was delighted with the recent takeover of Afghanistan by the Taliban. He sincerely believed that his country should be under Islamic law. He was proud that women there were now being educated the Taliban way and not how they were educated in the west.

When we got to my home, I thanked him for the ride and he thanked me for my business. After alighting, I saw him check that I got in through the apartment gates safely.

Though I felt unsettled after his discourse, I knew that debating with him over a perspective that he was extremely passionate about would have ended badly. In a weird way, I was thankful for having met him as it reminded me that we all have strong views and opinions we cling to, and I had the ability to choose to be civil and respectful despite the polar differences between us.

4. Are you being gentle with your words?
In 2007, Dr Fiona Moir, Dr Shailesh Kumar – from the University of Auckland – and I launched a website to help university students manage their stress and anxiety. This website was revolutionary at the time as there were no similar self-help resources available. This was way before the proliferation of smart phones and apps. The website contained talks on anxiety management, guided meditations and finding meaning.

Our team sent an email to the whole university to announce the launch, and I was deluged with congratulatory emails from the faculty and staff thanking us for the innovative resource. However, there was one email that stood out. It was from a mathematics professor who took exception to the fact that we had interviewed people who talked about Christianity, Islam, Hinduism and Buddhism. Our perspective was that many university students find meaning in religion, so rekindling their connection with their religious group might help them find peace and meaning. In his email, the professor called me unprintable names and slung insults. He made it clear that he believed that, as the university was a secular institution, I was misusing its funds.

I responded to his email kindly, avoiding harsh words, to express my differing opinion. I was conscious that using angry and hostile words would not appease him. We emailed each other a few times, to the point that I became anxious about opening my inbox. His email barrage against our team continued.

After a while, it dawned on me that this would be an endless exchange, so I sent him an email suggesting that we meet. Since I had caused the problem, I offered to pay for our coffees. His tone changed and he became very friendly in his next email. However, our busy schedules meant we never got to meet.

Writing a kind, gentle email when angry took a lot of effort. It required restraint and mindfulness of my hurt emotions. However, I knew that responding angrily, even if I could justify it, was not going to resolve the issue. Most probably, an equally abrasive email from me would have inflamed the conflict further.

I have also used this technique of showing kindness in digital speech in another tricky situation involving group chats. I was a member of a group chat with several thousand Filipinos in New Zealand, but I was usually a lurker there, reading threads and rarely contributing. Usual topics in this group included relocation issues, schools for children, where to find Filipino food, adjusting to living in New Zealand and visa issues.

One woman posted about her horrible experience of being racially discriminated against in her workplace. This topic triggered a flurry of responses, with some sharing their own experiences and others talking about how they have felt accepted in New Zealand. As someone who has been in New Zealand for close to two decades, I shared my experience of being accepted in all my workplaces, at clinics, hospitals and the university. The original poster became very angry at my response, stating that I was invalidating her experience, and that racial discrimination is rife in New Zealand and in other western countries.

Having learned from my experience with the mathematics professor, I personally messaged the woman, sought to offer an apology for my post having caused her anger and offered to meet her for coffee. I deliberately avoided messaging her in the group chat to avoid further inflaming the matter. She accepted my apology and was friendly to me (virtually) afterwards.

Listen to the emotion not just the words

I have counselled parents who have come to me upset and concerned that their young child is suicidal. When I ask them what has happened, many times the story is the same. Their five-year-old misbehaved. The parents told the child off. The child had a tantrum. The parents stood their ground. The child said, 'I want to die.' The parents then panicked that their child was suicidal.

Most of the time, young children are not really suicidal. When they get upset, they say the most horrible things to express their anger and frustration. Children are not that different from us, as we do the same thing, often unconsciously.

A good way to respond to people who say horrible things when upset is to identify and address the underlying emotion of upset and anger. Responding to the emotion that drives hurtful speech is smarter than focusing on the spiteful words that are said. This requires a lot of mindfulness and restraint, as we often reflexively respond to the words instead of the emotions.

When arguing with someone, we often respond to the words said. 'You told me I was an idiot, that's why I called you a moron ...'

Focusing on the angry words becomes endless and unproductive, which fuels further upset and rage on both sides. An alternative approach is, 'When you told me I was an idiot, I sensed that you were really upset with me. I am sorry you are upset. Is there anything I can do to help?'

Sometimes, further verbal engagement is futile and having space to decompress and recalibrate is wise: 'We are both upset, let's have a break and talk later. I want you to know that I still love you, though.'

Gentle speech is appreciative, encouraging and inspiring. Occasionally, it can also be transformative.

Carl

Running had always been my preferred fitness activity, but I developed a painful foot condition that prevented me from doing it, so, in my late forties, I decided to take up swimming. I deliberately chose it because it is gentle on the joints, so I knew that if I learned it well, it could be my sport right into old age.

When I started, I was not very skilled at swimming, and I was afraid of the deep part of the pool and the sea. I was lucky to have several coaches who never judged me and who supported me in my training. One of them has stood out though – Carl.

I have trained in the pool with Carl twice a week for years. He has also coached me in ocean swimming. He is not a big talker but when he says things, I listen. He has a knack for giving genuine compliments, which encourage me to practise more.

A couple of years ago, he said to me, 'Tony, that's a really good catch.' (The catch is the initial part of a freestyle stroke when the arm pulls the water backwards.) 'I can see you have been training hard on that. Now, if you can, concentrate on that good technique for the next six months ...'

Six months doing the same thing sounded daunting, but his words reverberated in my head when I trained alone in the pool. A few years later, I am still conscious of performing a good catch, stroke by stroke.

Two years ago, I asked Carl if he thought I was ready to do the Rangitoto crossing, an intimidating 4.6-kilometre ocean swim from Rangitoto Island to St Heliers in Auckland. He said, 'You're not ready for that yet, but continue doing your pool and ocean training, and you will be ready next year.'

A year later I asked Carl if I was ready and he said, 'Yes, you can do it.'

Just before jumping into the ocean to begin my race, I believed that I could do it because I trusted Carl's words. I swam the Rangitoto crossing successfully and credited Carl not just for the training but for his kind, gentle and inspiring words.

5. Is what you are about to say gossip?

The Buddha was explicit about gossip. 'What one has heard here is not repeated there, so as to cause dissension there. What one has heard there is not repeated here, so as not to cause dissension here.'

Gossip is defined as talking about other people who are not present. All humans gossip, as we talk about other people all the time. We talk about relatives, workmates, neighbours, politicians, religious people, historical personalities, celebrities and, most importantly, our in-laws! There have been some interesting studies on gossip that show that both men and women gossip and that most of the time, the gossip is neutral or benign and not negative.

There are theories as to why humans gossip. It results in social connection. We feel connected when we talk about others. It mitigates loneliness and fosters bonding. Gossip may also have the important function of disseminating stories, some of which may be valuable, for example, warning others not to let a particular person in the house as he has 'sticky fingers'.

It is the negative or destructive gossip that the Buddha suggests we avoid. It is gossip that causes dissent or disagreement. In a weird way, some people feel good or superior when they bad-mouth others.

In my first week working as a psychiatrist in New Zealand, I noticed a group of nurses and doctors standing around in the kitchen. They were laughing hysterically. Feeling intrigued, I walked slowly towards the group, trying to be subtle in my shuffle. One of them said, 'Tony, you're new here so you should listen to this.'

I felt good that they considered me part of their group, then a senior nurse came over and warned me to stay away from the group as they were gossiping. A few other staff walked away from the group at the same time. Despite the invitation to join, I decided to walk away as well. Later, I found out that they'd been talking about one of the clinic bosses in an unflattering light.

That was the first time I had seen people deliberately walk away from a gossip session. I was impressed but at the same time felt guilty because if it had not been for that senior nurse, I probably would have joined in the gossip too.

Gossiping is powerful and we are naturally drawn to it. Despite the Buddha's admonition to stay away from gossip, many of us will repeatedly engage in it unless we understand what it is that drives us to gossip. This requires a bit of curiosity and mindfulness as it is like detective work of our mind when we are about to gossip.

Self-reflection

Are you gossiping because you are angry at someone?

Are you gossiping because you want to feel good about yourself by putting others down?

Do you want to gossip because you are bored and need entertainment?

How would you feel if you reversed the scenario and found out that others were gossiping about you?

There have been a few instances when, during a gossip session, my mindfulness and compassion have kicked in. Instead of carrying on with the gossiping, I asked the group if there were other explanations for the alleged misbehaviour. Occasionally,

I asked my fellow gossipers if it was worth asking the person their side of the story. One way to douse cold water over a hot gossip session is to talk about some of the good things the person being talked about has done. On a few occasions, following the footsteps of that senior nurse, I have quietly walked out of a gossip session.

Noble silence

In a counterintuitive manner, practising noble silence and avoiding speech unless it is necessary for a day can help you develop kind speech. You can explain to your family that you are practising noble silence once a month as part of training to be kinder to others.

When you are quiet, you can see your thoughts and intentions with increased clarity. You can see your impulses to praise as well as pour scorn. You can see that the urge to comment just for wanting to say something is frequent.

When you have the urge to say something, ask yourself if what you are about to say is 100 per cent true. Is what you are about to say kind? Gentle? Purposeful? Timely? And will it lead to peace and happiness? Notice the urge to blurt things, just notice, then smile and it will go away (hopefully). With noble silence, you are strengthening your muscle of self-restraint, and the virtues of patience and of letting go.

CHAPTER 5

Precept two: harmlessness

Humans have an extraordinary capacity to care and show compassion for others. At the same time, humans can display astonishing cruelty to other humans and to animals. Even religious leaders who espouse kindness and godliness have inspired shocking viciousness in the form of bigotry, slavery, torture, oppression and genocide of non-believers for the sake of their gods and prophets.

In his teachings, the Buddha was unequivocal about not causing harm to any beings.

> *All tremble at violence;*
> *all fear death.*
> *Putting oneself in the place of another,*
> *one should not kill*
> *nor cause another to kill.*

The Buddha's urging for his followers to refrain from hurting others comes from a place of compassion. He knows that if we are threatened, shown violence, or physically harmed, we suffer immensely. It makes sense, then, for us to not do the same to others because of the suffering we will inflict on them.

Killing other people is considered one of the most harmful behaviours that humans can engage in. Killing a human causes incalculable harm to the victim and to that person's family, friends and community. Sometimes, the repercussion of murder is felt multiple generations after the act.

Human life is considered extremely precious in the Buddha's eyes. To illustrate this, there is a classic Buddhist story of an old, blind turtle who lives in the bottom of the world's oceans. This turtle surfaces once every 100 years. Floating somewhere randomly in the vast oceans is a yoke. Being born a human is rarer than the turtle raising its head through the yoke in its hundredth-year breath. Thus is the preciousness of human life.

Apart from destroying something extremely precious, the act of hurting or even killing living beings arouses a primal gut reaction of disgust in most of us. Our brains have evolved to experience disgust and horror when we witness such violence. Remember Hiri and Ottappa? Our conscience aches when see humans and animals tortured and harmed.

We all have the capacity to harm

· ·

Hack 14: If you have thoughts of harm to others, understand the trigger behind them.

· ·

The likelihood of you, a reader of this book, being involved in killing another person is extremely low. If, like my patient William, you killed someone, chances are a part of your being would know that what you had done was wrong, even if you felt that it was justified.

Though we might not actually kill another human being, many of us have had or will have homicidal fantasies. The desire to wish someone dead is not rare at all. In one study, the authors estimated that that the majority of research participants had had homicidal fantasies, with 77 per cent of men and 63 per cent of women reporting having had at least one homicidal fantasy. Men's homicidal fantasies tended to be more elaborate and detailed. Most thoughts of homicide are triggered by interpersonal conflict. The majority of these thoughts are brief and do not progress to detailed planning.

If, for some reason, you have thoughts of harming or killing someone else, reassure yourself that most probably you are just like any normal human being. Understanding what is triggering homicidal thoughts – usually anger, frustration or feeling threatened – is crucial in addressing the urge to harm.

Experiencing these strong emotions is part of being human. If you want peace and less suffering, there are other alternatives than violence to deal with powerful yet normal negative emotions.

Mary

Mary was a violinist in her thirties whose career was just starting to flourish; she was being invited to perform in concert halls all over the world. She lived with her mother, who had belittled her since she was a child. Mary's mother did not mince her words when telling her daughter she was ugly, no good and would never succeed in life. Her mother told her she would always be a second-rate violinist who would never be a famous soloist.

While Mary's career was blossoming, her mother developed an aggressive form of dementia. With all their other relatives living overseas, Mary became her mother's caregiver, and the verbal attacks intensified to become physical assaults. When upset, her mother bit and scratched Mary.

Mary came to see me when she started having panic attacks. She told me her panic attacks began when she started having fantasies of killing her mother. These included visual fantasies of suffocating her mother while she was asleep, overdosing her with sedatives or drowning her in the bath. She felt extremely guilty for having these thoughts.

Our therapy focused on understanding her complicated relationship with her mother, the lifelong abuse she had experienced and her desire to be free from her mother. We normalised her homicidal fantasies in that they were simply an expression of the anger and frustration that had built up through the decades.

Once she accepted that being extremely angry at her mother was normal given her experiences, Mary's panic attacks subsided. Moving her mother to a care facility further improved their relationship and she continued to visit weekly until her mother passed away.

Abstaining from killing is not limited to killing human beings

The Buddha's precept includes not killing animals that have consciousness. This includes all animals, whether they're mammals, reptiles, birds, insects or fish.

Buddhist monks and nuns take the precept of non-killing very seriously. In the Buddhist monastic code of rules, called the Vinaya, the Buddha explicitly detailed 227 rules and one of the most important precepts is 'no killing'. If a monk or nun deliberately and knowingly kills an animal, it is considered a serious downfall that requires powerful penance.

As a newly ordained Buddhist monk in Burma, I was extra neurotic about the rules, making sure I followed them and did not breach any of them. Even when mosquitoes landed and fed on my arm while meditating, I carefully flicked or blew them away, making sure I did not injure or squash them. This was not what I would have done before I became a monk.

For many of us, our natural tendency towards bugs and small animals we do not like is to exterminate them. We often see them as pests and low-lifes that do not deserve to live within our realm.

One morning, fresh from my ordination, I woke up and half-consciously walked to the bathroom. The bathroom floor was crawling with black ants! Without much thought, I filled a plastic pitcher with water and splashed the bathroom floor to get rid of the ants. Then I thought, 'Oh no! I am committing ant genocide and, of all places, in a Buddhist monastery.'

I got some tissue paper, rolled it up like a scooper, then went down on my knees to rescue all the ants I could see. I saved more than 100 ants but could not count how many had drowned.

As I'd caused the death of conscious animals, I discussed it with a senior nun, who examined the situation. She told me that as I'd acted without clear intention, I had not broken the Vinaya rules.

To breach the precept of non-killing, there must be a clear intention of wanting to kill, full knowledge that a being will be killed and that any action is motivated by wanting to take a life. Accidental killing of another being, for example stepping on ants or bugs crashing on the windshield, is not considered to breach the precept, as there is no intention to kill.

My good friend Rich is a keen fisherman. He enjoys the peace of being in a boat in the middle of the ocean, no phone, no internet, just sitting quietly, holding a fishing rod. I like the ocean but never imagined myself as a fisherman because I thought it would be boring.

One summer morning, he was able to organise a fancy boat and a few rods, and we went out fishing. He set up my bait and taught me how to hold the rod. In less than 10 minutes, I felt something nibbling on my bait. I carefully reeled in a snapper. It was gasping and flapping. We made eye contact. My heart was crushed, and I had to release it back to the water. I justified returning the snapper to the sea as it was smaller than the allowed length, but I don't think I can go fishing again. I enjoyed being in the boat in the middle of the ocean, but actively killing another creature would be too painful for me.

From the Theravadan tradition, the Buddha was not vegetarian, and he did not command his followers to be vegetarian. However, many followers of the Buddha's teachings eventually become vegetarian out of compassion for animals. There are many Buddhist traditions that are vegetarian and prohibit the killing of animals.

I was a guest in a Tibetan monastery outside Kathmandu where there were explicit rules regarding not eating meat and not killing any animals within the monastery grounds. However, when I was a monk in Burma, many of the monks ate all the food, including meat, offered by the community. The Dalai Lama is mostly vegetarian but, because of health problems, he eats meat once a week.

Though following the precept of non-harm is straightforward in day-to-day life, there are situations in which, despite our best intentions, following the precept becomes complicated. Take for example the case of a monastery plagued with termites. Non-harmful interventions did not work, so the abbot of the monastery made the painful decision to hire professional exterminators.

A common dilemma for Buddhists is the euthanasia of very ill and suffering pets. Should one prolong the life of a pet that is suffering just for the sake of following the precept of non-killing? Should one look at the importance of alleviating the suffering of the pet by allowing euthanasia? As a pet owner, ask yourself what the true motivation for euthanasia is. Is it to relieve the suffering of your pet or is to relieve your own suffering?

The precept of non-killing should not be followed blindly. Instead, the precept allows us to pause and deeply reflect on the various motivations at play. Based on one's deep reflection, hopefully guided by wisdom, a plan of action is decided.

In these controversial situations, the bottom line is that the precept of non-killing and harmlessness are guidelines and not commandments. Each case has to be viewed individually and carefully. Buddhist morality is not imposed by an outside authority. Our morality is imposed from within, from our felt sense of what is true.

· . · · . · · . · · · . · · . · · . · · . · · . · · . · · . · · . · · . · · ·

Hack 15: Consciously practising harmlessness softens the heart.

· . · · . · · · . · · . · · . · · . · · . · · . · · . · · . · · . · · . · · ·

What's in it for us if we avoid killing not just people but animals too? From my own experience, observing the precept of non-killing or non-harm of animals has made me more sensitive to the preciousness of life. Even a tiny insect like an ant is a marvel of nature that no human technology can replicate. Humankind has amassed incalculable wealth and superior scientific technology to the point that we have built spaceships that can cross the solar system and synthesised bombs that can annihilate all of humanity. Despite all of that, we still cannot replicate an ant or a bed bug.

Observing the precept of harmlessness even when there is a strong impulse to hurt develops within us patient endurance, a quality that is very useful in daily life.

If we regularly allow ourselves to give in to our inclination to kill bugs or harm other creatures, we risk developing a callous mindset that is insensitive to other creatures' suffering.

Being conscious of not harming or killing makes one aware that all creatures with consciousness (animals and humans) want the same things in life: food, water and safety. By regularly observing the precept of non-harm, the sense of connectedness and compassion is enhanced, which are both important conditions for happiness.

CHAPTER 6

The remaining precepts

Precept 3 – non-stealing

A few years ago, I went on a holiday to Paris. I checked in at a nice hotel across from the Sorbonne University. Even though I have been warned many times about thefts in certain European cities, I have my guard down once I am in a nice hotel. I unpacked my luggage, and put 400 euros, my spending money, on the dresser. After a quick shower, I left the hotel to pick up my sister from the airport. As I am cognisant of pickpockets, I only took 20 euros with me.

When I got back to the hotel, the 400 euros were gone. I was stunned. I spoke to the manager and told him what had happened. He confirmed that cleaners had been in my room. I thought that was a bit unusual as I had only arrived a couple of hours earlier. He got angry at me for insinuating that the cleaners had stolen my cash. I was emphatic that my cash had disappeared but I did not make any accusations. I could not prove the theft, but I felt that management should be aware of the incident.

After that experience and another incident in Madrid, my guard now goes up when I travel to certain cities. When strangers get close, I hold on tight to my backpack and I use a money belt to keep my passport and credit cards safe.

Conversely, travelling in Japan is a totally different experience. I feel very safe there as I know I will not be mugged or pickpocketed. The Japanese are very respectful of others and rates of thievery are low. If you lose your wallet with money inside, there is a more than 70 per cent chance that you will have it returned to you!

People steal for various reasons. Where there is poverty, much of the petty stealing is driven by economic hardship. Some people steal for the excitement of the act. Some steal because they believe the organisations they're stealing from are so wealthy that the theft doesn't matter at all. Some feel entitled to steal as their victim has wronged them. Then there are mental health reasons, like kleptomania, that push people to steal.

Many people will say that they have never stolen anything in their life. This is in contrast to some studies that show that as many as 70 per cent of employees have been involved in one type of theft or another. Work theft can be in the form of stealing merchandise, money or time. Around 15 per cent of teenagers have stolen.

Self-reflection

If you think you have not stolen anything, ask yourself:

- Have you taken home a pen or some office material that is not yours?
- Have you downloaded music or a movie from a pirate site?
- Have you used your paid time at work looking at social media or consciously doing non-work-related activities?

The Buddha would not have included non-stealing as a precept if theft was rare, or if the urge to take something not offered to us was uncommon.

The Buddha was clear about the precept of non-stealing: 'He avoids taking what is not given and abstains from it; what another person possesses of goods and chattel in the village or in the wood, that he does not take away with thievish intent.'

· ·

Hack 16: Respecting others' property cultivates restraint, patience and contentment. It makes people around you feel safe.

· ·

The Buddha instructed his disciples to respect what is not theirs for a reason. Practising non-stealing yields various fruits, which benefit followers of the precepts and those around them.

If people who live together all practise non-stealing, they feel safe with each other, which then enhances peace and harmony in the community. That's how I feel every time I'm in Japan!

However, when people feel they are easy prey for opportunists, thieves and robbers, there is a sense of mistrust that causes internal tension and a constant feeling of unease.

When one practises genuine respect for other people's property, one cultivates the virtue of contentment. We become satisfied with what we have. We learn that we do not need to acquire more stuff, especially if it is obtained unethically.

Not taking what is not on offer is practised regularly during mealtimes in Theravada Buddhist monasteries. Monks in

Theravada monasteries eat one main meal a day before midday and no more food for the rest of the day.

When I was a monk in Burma, I was already famished at dawn because my last meal had been before noon the previous day. By lunch time, the craving for food was at its most intense. In the afternoons and evenings, we were allowed certain drinks but no food or solids.

Before my monk training, I ate three substantial meals a day with absolute regularity. I would get upset and even develop headaches if I did not eat on time. The whole monastery eating schedule was quite a challenge for a foodie like me.

To signal lunch time, a bell rang and the monks quietly queued according to seniority. As I was the newest ordained monk, I was at the back of the queue. Monks then slowly walked from the assembly area to the dining hall. By this time, all I could think was, 'Hurry up, I am so hungry!'

We then gathered around our assigned tables, which were full of delectable dishes donated from the community. Being so hungry and kneeling quietly in front of the banquet felt like torture. I had a strong impulse to grab a morsel and gobble it as inconspicuously as possible.

The head monk sang a thanksgiving chant ... slowly. After the chant, we still couldn't eat. A layperson had to go around the tables offering the various foods to the monks. If the food was not offered to us, we could not eat as, technically, they were not ours. This was excellent daily training for following the precept of non-stealing, of not taking what is not offered. Waiting to eat food an arm's length in front of you when famished is also a superb drill for mindfulness. With calm attention, I watched hunger pangs, impatience and strong thoughts of wanting to steal a piece of chicken and stuff it in my mouth.

Having experienced life as a monk several times and attended various Buddhist retreats, I am less attached to food. I still love food and think about food a lot but much less than I did before. I can survive having just one meal a day. I can see cookies and chocolate in the pantry without a strong urge to eat them. Surprisingly, my hunger-induced migraines have also disappeared.

Precept 4 – Avoiding sexual misconduct

When I take a thorough medical and psychiatric history of a patient, I ask them about experiences of sexual abuse and violence. After 20 years of clinical practice, I am no longer surprised by the huge number of my patients, both male and female, who report sexual abuse when they were children, teenagers and even as adults. The experience of sexual abuse and trauma has been shown to have strong links to future experiences of psychiatric conditions including depression, anxiety, eating disorders, post-traumatic stress disorder, sleep disorders and suicide attempts.

Looking at the data from a 2015 study by the United States' National Sexual Violence Resource Center on the frequency of sexual violence is a sobering exercise: one in five women and one in 71 men will be raped at some point in their life. In 80 per cent of rape cases, the perpetrator is known to the victim. One in four girls and one in six boys will be sexually assaulted before they turn 18, and 34 per cent of the abusers are family members.

Apart from rape, sexual assault and other forms of sexual violence, another type of sexual misconduct is having sexual relations with those who are in committed relationships. Infidelity is one of the most common causes of divorce, as many couples are not able to bounce back once cheating has occurred in the relationship. If you are in a relationship, a common source of stress and conflict is the concern that your partner is cheating on you.

Given the Buddha's wisdom, he was probably aware of the extent that sexual misconduct occurred in society and the damage it wrought not just on the victims but on the perpetrators themselves.

To the monks, he said, 'He avoids sexual misconduct and abstains from it. He has no intercourse with such persons as are still under the protection of father, mother, brother, sister or relatives, nor with married women, nor with female convicts, nor lastly with betrothed girls.' A similar directive was provided to women.

This precept on sexual misconduct aims to protect people in relationships and to promote loyalty, trustworthiness and honesty in unions. In addition, the precept also considers coerced, aggressive and deceitful sexual activities as transgressions.

In short, sexual relations that cause harm to participants breaks the precept. On the other hand, having sexual relations with another consenting adult who is unattached is not considered sexual misconduct.

All of the precepts aim to cultivate serenity and harmony in relationships, families and communities. If we want to be happy, feeling safe, secure and unthreatened is crucial. Sexual misconduct does the opposite. In addition to potentially causing discord, the negative effects on the happiness of the people involved are often incalculable.

The main driver for sexual misconduct is lust or sexual desire. Most adult humans experience sexual desire, as it is important for the propagation of the species.

Unlike that of other religious groups, from a Buddhist perspective, there is nothing wrong with having sexual desire. It is just another form of desire, no different from the desire to eat, drink, be famous, acquire possessions, be happy, be comfortable or have more likes on Facebook. We have endless lists of desires, but it is how we deal with our desires that can cause problems.

Nowadays in the west, giving in to one's sexual desire is much easier than it once was. Society is more permissive and less judgmental when it comes to sexual orientation and sexual behaviours. In most cases, it is no longer difficult to satisfy one's sexual cravings, whether in a solo activity or with other people. As of 2022, there were at least 1500 dating apps, which can be used to find casual sexual partners. At any given second, one of the most popular pornography websites has 1000 visitors, which adds up to 78 million visits per day.

The seeming paradox is despite increasing methods and access to satisfy sexual desires, the demand does not seem to decrease at all.

Hack 17: Constant feeding of desire does not satisfy the desire.

Lust, like any desire, can be temporarily eased but it does not go away. When scratching an itch from a bug bite, there is momentary relief, but the itch can come back with a vengeance, especially if the toxin has been spread by the scratching. Constantly satisfying the desire can fuel the desire further.

I have treated a few cases of people whose sexual desires have become excessive and problematic. Their stories are very similar in that they initially found giving in to their sexual desires both exciting and satisfying, albeit temporarily. However, they eventually indulged in their preferred sexual activity with such frequency that it got out of control. They reached a point that giving in to their sexual desires did not give them pleasure anymore, but they were unable to stop the behaviour, which had acquired a life of its own. Despite not getting the same amount of pleasure they'd had in the beginning, they had become chained to the compulsive behaviours.

I once had a patient who was a young, fine-looking tennis player. He was gregarious, friendly and likeable. Despite his warm and happy exterior, he constantly felt empty and unloved. He found temporary solace in meeting girls for casual sex at parties and in pubs. He then found meeting girls in person boring and tedious, so he met girls anonymously on dating apps.

After a few months, he found casual sex with women too easy and unstimulating, so he became engaged in various fetishes to keep the excitement up. He later got involved in sadism and masochism, where he found pleasure in hurting his sexual partners. He became worried that his sexual desires were getting out of control, as his sexual fantasies now involved various types of violence. It was then that he sought professional assistance. His sexual activities had started to cause harm not just to others but to his own mental health as well.

From a Buddhist perspective, my young patient and others who become addicted to sex are not deviants or evil people. They are people just like us who have desires, except their desires have got out of control. They are not different from people who have become addicted to alcohol, drugs, food, shopping, money or fame. *They* are not the problem; sexual desire is not the problem – their uncontrolled desire is the problem.

A student once said to Zen master Suzuki Roshi, 'Roshi, I have a lot of sexual desire. When I sit I just get more sexual desire. I try to concentrate on my practice. I'm thinking of becoming celibate. Should I limit myself in this way?'

Suzuki answered, 'Sex is like brushing your teeth. It's a good thing to do but not so good to do it all day long.'

Buddhism is not anti-sex. It recognises that sexual desires are normal. Laypeople can engage in sexual activities as long as they are consensual and do not cause harm to themselves or others. In fact, Ajahn Maha Boowa, a Thai Buddhist master, commented that sex in a partnership is like an oven in a kitchen: 'Both are necessary to establishing and maintaining a successful family.'

Buddhism offers various practical techniques for managing uncontrolled desires, including sexual desire or lust.

Hack 18: Mindfulness can help manage excessive desire.

Mindfulness is key to working with desires. It involves being fully present with the experience in an accepting and non-judgmental manner. If sexual desires come up, don't make too big a fuss about it, just notice them come and go. Engaging with the story feeds it. Try not to complicate it by judging yourself and thinking that you are a bad person, or that you are a sex addict or a deviant.

Most of us have sexual desires but worrying about them or suppressing them can make them more intense. Paying attention to the breath or focusing on other bodily sensations may help. Changing activities by going out for a walk, reading, having a chat with a friend, or engaging in physical exercise can also help. Eventually, just as other desires we have do, lust goes away.

A friend who grew up in a strict Irish Catholic family was given instructions by a priest on how to manage his intense sexual thoughts. In certain parts of the Catholic church, entertaining sexual fantasy is considered a mortal sin – a sin against God, which may result in eternal damnation. He was told that entertaining a sexual fantasy without even acting on the thought could be considered adultery.

My friend tried all sorts of techniques to banish his strong sexual thoughts. He tried praying, splashing ice water on his face and genitals, and at one point, he resorted to beating himself with a whip. None of these strategies worked. The more heroic his effort to banish them, the stronger the sexual thoughts became. He then met another priest who had had extensive mindfulness meditation training. This priest told him to not worry about the thoughts as they were normal, especially given that he was a young man.

Noticing the thoughts when they arose and acknowledging them as that – just thoughts that arise and pass away – coupled with calming breathing techniques worked. The thoughts never went away but their intensity and ferocity became manageable.

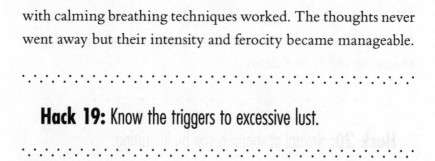

Hack 19: Know the triggers to excessive lust.

Understanding the triggers for excessive lust can also help target ways to manage it. Common triggers include alcohol, pornography and certain mental states.

Cutting back on excessive alcohol use or not having alcohol in the house can help.

Eliminating pornography by blocking websites can delay the access to them by a few steps.

Feelings of loneliness or boredom can be mindfully recognised, understood and accepted as normal states.

Distraction or engaging in healthier activities like connecting with non-sexual friends will facilitate the reduction of sexual desires.

Alcoholics Anonymous uses the motto 'One day at a time'. When using it, members promise not to drink today. Promising not to drink for a week, a month or the rest of one's life is too scary and unrealistic. But for today, it is possible. Abstaining from sexual misconduct can be approached in the same way. One can make a commitment to abstain for a day, as that is achievable and realistic.

Another strategy is to shift how we relate to people we desire sexually. A technique taught by Buddhist teachers is to view all women as our sisters, all men as our brothers, older people as our parents and younger people as our children.

Self-centred lust can transform to empathy and genuine concern if we see others as family and friends and not as objects to satisfy our desire.

· ·

Hack 20: Sexual abstinence can be liberating.

· ·

Lust is a powerful desire and, if uncontrolled, it can be a hindrance to feeling content. Lust can destroy inner peace. As long as we are alive, these desires will always be there, as they are part of being human.

When I investigate my past experiences in satisfying my desires, for example, the desire to eat ice cream, I realise that, despite the hundreds of gallons of ice cream I have consumed in 50 years, I still desire ice cream. I have eaten the best ice creams I can lay my hands on, but I still want ice cream. Most probably, I will still be wanting ice cream on my deathbed. The desire for sex is the same.

Even if you have had the most exciting sex life ever and have fulfilled all your sexual fantasies, chances are your desire has never been fully satisfied and you want more.

Knowing that ignorant and uncontrolled desires cause internal suffering, many followers of the Buddha decide to abandon sexual desires by becoming celibate. Some commit to abstaining from sexual activity for a day, a week or years. For Buddhist monks and nuns, they commit to sexual abstinence indefinitely while they are still in robes. They have realised that indulgence in their desire does not really take away the desire.

I must make it clear that the Buddha never commanded celibacy. Relative to other religious leaders, the Buddha was relaxed about sex, particularly for laypeople. Celibacy is just another lifestyle option for everyone, not that different from a decision to abstain from alcohol, meat or sweets. Some of the Buddha's followers deliberately choose to be celibate, as celibacy weakens the grip of sexual desire on the mind. For those who commit to celibacy, some find it a straightforward decision while many, even famous Buddhist masters, struggle for a few years before they achieve it.

Commitment to celibacy frees up the mind from the constant planning, organising and fantasising of sexual activities. Relationships and friendships become more straightforward as there is no second-guessing what is going on with other people's minds or intentions.

For monks and nuns who dedicate their lives to cultivating positive mental states and liberation from greed and desire, celibacy is essential in their training. Sri Lankan meditation master Bhante Gunaratana says that, as a celibate, the preoccupation on satisfying one's sensual pleasures is less and there is more room for a more compassionate heart that is not a slave to craving's call.

Precept 5 – Avoiding intoxicants

James

James was a devout member of a Christian church in a small New Zealand town. He had been active in the church community since he was a young boy, as his father was a church elder. To celebrate a good friend's twenty-fifth birthday, James went to the city with a large group of friends. He rarely drank alcohol but this night was extra special so he had a few gin and tonics, half a dozen bottles of beers and some tequila.

From a usually soft-spoken, shy and kind man, he transformed to an obnoxious and aggressive drunk. He had a fight with another drunk patron, and they both got kicked out of the bar. He then went back to his hotel, where he was accused by a female friend of being sexually aggressive towards her.

Afterwards, James had poor recollection of the evening's events, but a video of him being belligerent in the bar went viral on social media. His reputation was in tatters. He lost his job as a trainee mechanic and was disowned by his father.

James's story is not rare. Problematic alcohol use is on the rise. Up to half of men who commit violence have problems with alcohol. A study of close to 17,000 US inmates showed that alcohol had played a significant role in various crimes, including homicide, physical violence, sexual violence, robbery and burglary. An interesting finding was that even moderate amounts of alcohol were associated with violence.

Long-term use of alcohol changes an individual's ability for self-control, decision-making and emotional processing. Alcohol is just one of many substances implicated in violent behaviours. Others include cocaine, cannabis, opioids and methamphetamine.

Even though the Buddha lived 2600 years ago, he was familiar with the effects of recreational substances on humans: 'A noble disciple gives up wines, liquors and intoxicants, the basis for negligence, and abstains from them. By abstaining from wines, liquors and intoxicants, the noble disciple gives to immeasurable beings freedom from fear, hostility and oppression ... he himself will enjoy immeasurable freedom from fear, hostility and oppression.'

A follower of the Buddha who is clear-headed and not intoxicated is more careful in their thoughts, speech and actions. They give the gift of safety to others.

When we are intoxicated or disinhibited by chemicals, we are less aware of what is right and wrong. Our cognitive filters become porous, and we are more prone to acting impulsively. This can lead us to say unmentionable things to friends, family and strangers. Worse, we might act out our aggressive impulses that are otherwise under control when we are sober.

'The one who drinks this brew will sin in thought, word and deed. He will see good as evil and evil as good. Even the most modest person will act indecently when drunk. The wisest man will babble foolishly.'

The Buddha did not wholly ban the use of chemicals that affect the mind. Proper use of narcotics or pain medications do not breach the precept. However, if one were to follow the Buddha's precept on intoxicants strictly, any amount of alcohol is not accepted.

This is particularly relevant for people who are trying to give up drugs and alcohol in 12-step programmes like Alcoholics Anonymous or Narcotics Anonymous, for whom clarity around this point and the encouragement towards complete abstinence is especially important.

Similarly, recreational substances like cannabis and hallucinogens are discouraged in traditional Buddhist schools, while some western Buddhists have a more relaxed attitude towards them.

An important question to ask is what drives people to use recreational substances. The majority of drinkers find alcohol and other intoxicants relaxing. After a stressful day at work, a bottle of beer is like a treat that relaxes the mind.

For some, however, chemicals do not just result in a temporary relief from stress. Alcohol and other recreational substances make them feel normal or complete. I have seen this with some of my patients who have depression and anxiety. Alcohol and other chemicals make them feel whole, which puts them at risk for using them regularly.

Simply abstaining from intoxicants can be extremely difficult for these folks, as these chemicals make them feel normal again. Just stopping is not realistic and can sometimes be dangerous. Availing of programmes including Alcoholics Anonymous or other substance-abuse interventions may be necessary for them to be liberated from the clutches of intoxicants.

The chemicals themselves are not the problem. The potential harmful effects of the chemicals are the main concern. Substances can cause heedlessness and carelessness, which can lead to harmful speech and actions. These can then disrupt relationships and cause harm to others and oneself. If we truly want to gift safety to others around us, having a clear, lucid and rational mind is essential.

Hack 21: If you want a clear mind, avoid intoxication.

Training for a marathon involves at least five to six months of preparation, several runs a week and hundreds of hours pounding the pavement. As marathon training requires a pair of well-functioning lungs, smoking is strongly discouraged. Similarly, training our minds to be clear, rational and happy requires a lot of effort and sacrifice on our part. Avoiding intoxication is like avoiding smoking. If you want clear lungs, avoid smoking. If you want a clear mind, avoid intoxication.

Bringing the precepts together

· ·

Hack 22: Not giving in to all of your urges is good for you.

· ·

At lunch, John was telling me how exhausted he was after spending the morning with his gym buddy. They lifted heavy weights for two hours, but it wasn't the 200-kilogram bench presses that exhausted John. It was being with his friend that tired him out completely. His friend constantly made negative comments about everyone – people in the gym, his family, his friends, people in government. His friend was unable control his urge to complain and whinge and finished every sentence with expletives.

Many of us have the urge to moan and complain. Not only that, but we have other urges too. We have the urge to defend the car park we feel is ours, the urge to uphold our political views when challenged, the urge to toot the horn when the car in front of us is not moving one second after the light turns green.

On a more basic level, we have the urge to look at people we find attractive, the urge to touch different items when we are in a clothing shop, to smell the various colognes at the duty-free store in the airport, to try all the different desserts in a buffet even if we are full.

Many of us have become slaves to our phones. We have the urge to constantly pick them up when we are bored, which seems to be every few minutes. The average phone use now is more than three hours per day per person, and it is increasing.

Some urges when not controlled can cause us problems, like the urge to have more alcohol after the first glass, or the urge to become violent when we are upset.

Observing the precepts is a good training ground to calm those urges. When I have the urge to make an unhelpful comment or to express my disapproving thoughts, I notice the urge and remember the precept of kind speech.

When I have the urge to squash the straggler ant inside my newly vacuumed car, I remember the precept of harmlessness and the gift of safety.

Western culture now highly regards indulgence. Give in to all our urges and desires, advertisers say. Sadly, for many, we aim for a life where we can give in to all our desires and cravings. That is supposed to be utopia – but is it? I think it sounds more like a recipe for chaos and anarchy.

Being conscious of the precepts allow us to practise restraint, a word rarely used nowadays. Another term for restraint is delayed gratification.

A famous series of studies on delayed gratification were conducted at Stanford University in the 1970s. In them, children were given a choice of being given one cookie immediately, or, if they could wait for 15 minutes, they would be given two cookies.

Studies have shown that, in the future, the children who delayed eating their cookies had better self-control and performed better in terms of their physical and emotional health. Those who delayed gratifying their urges were also more successful financially.

Practising the precepts regularly trains us to calm our urges and delay instant pleasure for something better in the future.

CHAPTER 7

Generosity

So far in my Buddhist journey, I have been ordained as a temporary monk four times – twice in Burma and twice at a Burmese monastery in Auckland, New Zealand. Temporary ordinations, which can last for a few days to months, are common in the Theravada Buddhist countries of Burma, Thailand, Sri Lanka and Laos.

My brief times spent as a monk have all been unforgettable experiences that I will treasure until I die. However, there was one aspect of being a Buddhist monk in Burma that has eclipsed all other memorable experiences as a monk.

In Burma, Buddhist monks and nuns typically do their alms rounds at dawn. Monks fold their robes in a complex 'formal' manner, which I never mastered. We transformed our upper robes into some sort of a turtleneck, long-sleeve garb that covered as much of the skin on our upper bodies as possible. I was told that apart from having a modest look, the intricate process was also some sort of security procedure that helped detect fake monks.

The folding procedure was such an elaborate process that I needed assistance from other monks every morning. Sometimes, it took them 10 minutes to wrap me up.

Once we were garbed properly, we lined up according to seniority, with the most senior monks in front and me second to last. The monk behind me was probably assigned to make sure I didn't get lost or distracted. He also kept an eye on my regularly unravelling upper robe.

Our alms bowls were big, round and metallic – the size of a basketball. The base had netting connected to a strap. We slung the bowls around our necks and held them in front of our bellies with both of our hands.

The monastery gate opened, and a young boy hit the flat brass bell every few seconds to announce to the village that the monks were coming out to collect food. There were around 20 of us walking solemnly, barefoot on the unpaved roads of the village. Sometimes, there were sharp rocks and occasionally rubbish that we had to navigate around carefully and mindfully.

Along our route, which covered a few kilometres, villagers lined up, waiting keenly to give food to the monks. Without making eye contact, we took the lids off our bowls and angled them to make sure food was not spilled on the pavement. Villagers were often barefoot, mostly standing, some kneeling, to show respect to Buddha's disciples. Most of the villagers gave us a spoonful of rice and small plastic bags of curry, soup or stir fry. Some more affluent villagers gave pots of food that our lay (non-monk) volunteers collected at the end of the procession.

As an extremely curious first-timer, my mind was assaulted by all kinds of thoughts and worries.

My upper robe was unravelling and my abdomen was starting to show. What should I do? I didn't know how to fix my robes, and with my hands on my bowl I couldn't do anything anyway. Fortunately, the monk behind me occasionally stopped me and fixed my robes. In my mind, I called him my fashion assistant as he always made sure my robes were properly folded and covered my torso throughout our alms rounds.

In one unmindful moment, I dropped the metal lid of my alms bowl. It made a loud bang, then rolled down the road! My fashion assistant monk and I chased it successfully and, pretending nothing happened, rejoined the procession.

Apart from constantly thinking about 'me' – Am I doing things right? Is my robe modestly folded? Am I walking mindfully? – what I will never forget is the generosity of the villagers. Most of them were poor, with a few families living in shack-like abodes made of scraps of wood and iron sheets. All of them keenly gave us some of their precious food.

Two young girls, probably aged seven or eight, rushed towards me with their offering. They knelt in front of me, gently bowed and put a packet of instant noodles in my bowl. Then, an old, hunched man with tattered clothes and a straw hat offered me a small banana. By this time, I could not stop my tears from flowing. I had never seen such generosity.

To outsiders, particularly capitalist-oriented westerners, this practice often seems bizarre. Giving food to monks every day does not make sense to them. Instead, they think these people should be saving their money and their food. However, from a villager's perspective, giving a little bit of their precious food first thing in the morning is the highlight of their day. I was even told that some villagers became very upset when the monks didn't pass along their road.

The practice of offering food and other small acts of kindness is the norm in many Buddhist countries. As such, it becomes second nature for people to share part of themselves even with strangers. Without the generous daily gift of food from the villagers, the monks would not be able to survive and practise the Buddha's teachings.

Despite being one of the poorest countries in the world, Burma often places in the top of the world leaderboard for generosity, besting some of the wealthiest countries in the world. Despite being materially poor, Burma is wealthy in terms of generosity.

What is generosity?

Generosity is the readiness to give. It is the motivation to contribute or support. The keyword is motivation, which is an intention to share or help. Generosity goes beyond what is expected in a standard financial transaction. In a western economic exchange, I pay $5 for a cup of cappuccino. If I'm feeling generous, I might add another dollar as a tip, which is not expected here in New Zealand. However, in the US, $1 might be the minimum tip expected so giving $2 would be considered generous.

Generosity is not limited to financial or material assistance. It can come in the form of attention, acknowledgment, time, service, thoughts or words. After receiving my cappuccino, I can be generous with a kind comment like, 'Thank you for making me coffee, it keeps me awake and focused for the morning!'

Giving generously – called 'dana' in Pali – is one of the most important human values a follower of the Buddha must develop. Westerners often equate Buddhist practice with meditation, but in traditionally Buddhist countries, Buddhism begins with generous giving and living harmlessly.

Giving generously is considered foundational, a strong base on which other practices like meditation can be built. It is said that the Buddha began many of his teachings by talking about generosity. From generosity, he talked about non-harmful or ethical behaviours, and only then did he talk about meditation. I do not think this is accidental. The Buddha said, 'To avoid evil, to cultivate the good and to purify one's mind, this is the teaching of all the Buddhas.'

Ethical behaviour comes before purifying the mind in meditation.

In his incredible wisdom, the Buddha knew that talking about and practising generosity warms the heart, which allows a student to be more open to further teachings and higher-level practices.

Systematic giving chips away at our natural tendency to be greedy and to focus excessively on the self, which often leads to suffering and discontentment. It is also possible that the Buddha thought that many of his followers would not be able to practise meditation or develop high levels of wisdom, but if they could just practise generosity and nothing else that person would have a joyful life at the very least.

Emphasising the importance of giving, the Buddha said, 'If people only knew the value of giving as he does, they would not take a single meal without sharing their food with others.'

Even deliberately giving a grain of rice to insects or birds is considered significant in the eyes of the Buddha.

There was a story of the Buddha being fed generously by Suppavasa, a noble female follower. After he finished his meal, the Buddha extolled the woman for her generosity. The Buddha said that with her generous food-giving, she had given beauty, long life, happiness and strength to those she fed. At the same time, by generously giving food to others, she herself would gain beauty, long life, happiness and strength.

· ·

Hack 23: Try giving without expecting anything in return, not even a thank you. You already benefit just by giving.

· ·

To give generously means that the intention is to benefit others. It is done out of compassion and a genuine wish that others be well and be free from suffering. Ideally, nothing is expected after one has given. Expectations can be in the form of being acknowledged or thanked, privately or publicly, or having the favour returned.

I said 'ideally nothing is expected', but it is very human to have some expectation after giving. Expecting to be thanked or recognised is not necessarily a selfish motivation but might have an evolutionary advantage. There are theories that generous individuals or species tend to fare better in terms of survival and propagation of the species.

However, expecting something in return can dampen the benefits one receives from being generous. If there is an expectation to be thanked or recognised or for a favour to be returned in the future, the generous act becomes more of a transactional exchange – 'I do this for you, you do this for me' – rather than genuine generosity. The benefit of giving, which is chipping away at the ego, is muted by expecting something in return.

In *Path to Enlightenment in Tibetan Buddhism*, Geshe Acharya Thubten Loden says that '... neither the gift nor the physical action of giving determine the perfection of generosity. The main thing is the mind. When you have become completely familiar, from the depths of your heart, with a willingness to give everything you possess, including the merit accumulated by such giving, you will have completed the perfection of generosity.'

It is taught that one who has perfected generosity feels immense joy whenever asked to give anything, even their own eyes.

Giving something that is of no value to the giver is simply giving but it is not generous giving. However, generous giving that results in harm to the giver is also discouraged.

After being allowed to stay in Chanmyay Myaing Monastery in Yangon as a temporarily ordained monk for two weeks, with free accommodation, free food and lots of pampering from the nun assigned to me, I decided to donate. There were no reminders or even expectations that I should give a donation.

Being an overthinker, I was in pain trying to calculate how much to give. I was hugely grateful for my amazing stay and was evaluating how much it would have cost me if I'd stayed in a nice hotel for two weeks in Burma. At the same time, I couldn't give so much that I wouldn't have enough funds for the rest of my trip.

I asked the nun assigned to me if she could give me a ballpark figure as to what people in my situation had donated. Looking at me with smiling eyes, she said, 'Give something that is not too little that it means nothing, but not too much that it causes harm.'

It still took me a while to decide how much to donate.

'Giving the best of what we have, instinctively and graciously, even if none remains for ourselves' is what the Buddha taught. We are only temporary caretakers of all that is provided.

Essentially, we own nothing. As this understanding takes root in us, there is no getting, possessing and giving – there is just the spaciousness that allows all things to remain in the natural flow of life.

From a Buddhist perspective, generous giving, which involves open-hearted letting go, is a potent antidote to the suffering that is caused by clinging and grasping not just to material objects but also to expectations, ideas, opinions, routines and concepts about I, me or mine. For a few seconds, while in the act of generous giving, our mind is liberated from its natural tendency for self-absorption and basks in the glow of kindness and connectedness with others.

Generosity in animals

Humans don't have a monopoly on generosity. Generous or selfless behaviours that benefit others have been documented in various species in the animal kingdom. One form of what we believe to be generosity in animals is food sharing. This differs from animals eating together as there is purposeful transfer of food from one motivated animal to a recipient.

Classic examples of food sharing can be seen in bees, ants and termites. These social insects are known for their altruistic tendency to forego reproduction and devote their life to serving and feeding their queen and/or colony.

In his study of vampire bats, Gerald Wilkinson found that they share food (blood) with other bats that are at risk of starvation and death. Vampire bats need to have blood from prey regularly, and if they do not feed in three days, they will lose body weight and eventually die. Vampire bats have been documented to donate blood they have collected to younger bats that are related to them as well as to non-related pups. They have also been shown to share blood with unrelated adult bats that have not fed and are at risk of death.

Food sharing among different types of primates has been documented in various forms. Mature primates have been known to share food with young ones. Males share with females, and females share with males. Primates also share food with others who they are not related with by blood. In the laboratory, bonobos, a primate species very close to chimpanzees and humans, have been recorded sharing nuts with each other even though there is no obvious benefit to them.

From an evolutionary perspective, food sharing has helped certain species survive and propagate. It is reasonable to assume that human generosity has a similar evolutionary basis, that generosity helped with the social organisation, propagation and sustenance of the species.

Scientists have tried to unlock what happens in our brains when we are generous. Some clues have been obtained from brain-imaging research on rhesus monkeys. Scientists have documented that when rhesus monkeys decide to share fruit juice in the laboratory, their brain shows synchrony of the amygdala and the medial prefrontal cortex. When the monkeys decide to be selfish and not share their juice, their brains show suppression of the synchrony. It seems that generosity or selfishness has a certain brain-wave signature.

Neuroscience

There have been multiple studies on humans and generosity. Recently, brain-imaging work has been done on humans who engage in generous intentions. Scientists from Germany, the

USA and Switzerland collaborated and asked the question, 'Does making a commitment to give generously make participants happy?'

The investigators started with 50 research participants who were randomly assigned to either the experimental or control group. Participants were informed that they would receive 25 Swiss francs (around US$30) weekly for the next four weeks. The participants in the experimental group were asked to commit to spending the money on other people of their own choice, which included taking others out for a meal or buying them gifts. The participants in the control group were asked to commit to spending the money on themselves. Several measurements were taken, including happiness scores and functional brain imaging.

Participants who committed to spending money on others reported higher happiness scores. Their brains also showed more significant changes in the brain networks associated with happiness than those in the control group. The main takeaway from this study is that a commitment or an intention to be generous results in happiness even before the actual behaviour takes place. Our brains experience happiness when we think thoughts of generosity.

Oxytocin is a hotly researched brain chemical. It has been nicknamed the 'cuddle' or 'love' hormone. It is released by the brain when we experience positive social interactions. We get a surge of oxytocin when we pet animals, and when we feel safe and surrounded by people we like. Our brain gets bathed with oxytocin when we hug, kiss and are intimate. Discharge of oxytocin causes positive emotional states including a feeling of trust, connection, relaxation, fondness and calm.

Oxytocin has also been linked to generous behaviour. In one study, oxytocin was administered through a nasal spray after which study participants were 80 per cent more likely to give generously, compared to those who received a placebo. The same study showed that participants who donated to charities had increased activation in parts of the brain rich with oxytocin receptors.

. . . .

Hack 24: Material generosity takes various forms. What is important is the desire to be of benefit to others.

. . . .

In 2020, Pete Kadens, a successful businessman from Ohio, informed graduating seniors of an impoverished public high school in Toledo that their college or trade school tuition would be paid for. In addition, one of each student's parents could also apply for a scholarship. The scholarships included not only tuition fees but also room and board, books and other costs, which increased the likelihood of the students achieving their degrees. Initially, the programme benefited around 100 families, but it has now been expanded to Chicago, with an ambitious goal of sending 30,000 students to college. Kadens has spent US$15 million of his own money and estimates reveal that he is using a disproportionately generous amount of his net worth with the charity.

I am still stunned by Kadens' generosity not just because of the cost to him but also the incalculable benefits his generosity will have. The thousands of lives he has impacted will be difficult to measure as the positive impacts will continue for several generations.

Most of us do not have the financial wealth of Pete Kadens but this does not mean we cannot be materially generous. On the other end of the spectrum, I know of parents in some struggling families who happily forgo meals just to make sure their children can eat. Some social experiments studying homeless people show how they willingly share precious food and even money with actors who pretend to be hungry and penniless.

Master Sheng Yen recounts a story of the Buddha as he was about to give a talk in the forest. It was getting dark. Many people offered their lamps but there was a homeless woman who offered her begging bowl, her only possession, to serve as an oil lamp. The Buddha announced to the crowd that this woman was most virtuous as she had offered her total wealth, her begging bowl.

Apart from making financial donations to individuals, organisations and charities, we can be materially generous in little things. We can be generous by buying a colleague a cup of coffee or giving an extra tip to our café server. Some of the women at our local monastery make a point of ensuring that the Buddha's shrine has fresh flowers every week. Even sharing some of your lunch with those you are dining with, if offered with an open heart, is a deeply generous act.

To make sure that I practise generosity regularly and not just based on impulse or emotion, I make monthly automatic payments to three organisations that I believe do a lot of good in our society, UNICEF, KidsCan – a New Zealand children's charity that feeds 50,000 poor Kiwi kids daily – and a local Burmese Buddhist monastery that performs many social work functions for Burmese migrants in Auckland.

One afternoon, while I was waiting to give a lecture in Wellington, I found myself wandering around the city's shops. In front of a supermarket was a smiley, dishevelled gentleman with an Irish shamrock design on his cap. He was sitting cross-legged on the cold pavement asking for coins. I asked him if he wanted me to get him anything at the supermarket. He said, 'Just a loaf of bread, please.'

I went inside and focused on making sure I got what he asked for and more. In addition to the loaf of bread, I got him butter, a roast chicken, a chocolate bar, juice and some ice cream. He was stunned and was profusely grateful. I warned him that there was ice cream in the bag and to make sure he ate it before it melted. It cost me no more than $30 but his gratitude was priceless. I was also grateful that he allowed me to practise generosity! It is a two-way process.

Material generosity is not all about money or buying things. It can come in the form of sharing possessions with an open heart, say by offering people car rides or sharing food.

One of my favourite generosity practices is feeding the birds in my backyard. Being Filipino, a lot of my meals include rice. When there is leftover rice in the fridge, I scatter it around the lawn and, as soon as I head back to the house, I can see the scout sparrows checking to see if it's safe for them to land. In less than 30 seconds (yes, I have timed it!) there will be at least 10 sparrows having a feast. In a minute or two, a few myna birds and blackbirds will join in. Occasionally, a starling or a neighbouring pigeon will visit.

I watch them from a distance, to make sure they feel safe. While watching them eat, my heart glows. I hope that they benefit from my gift, even for a short while. I feel that the local bird population knows me. They know that when I walk to the backyard with a pot, they are about to have another meal.

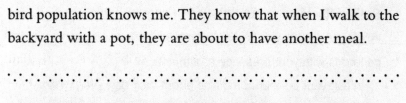

Hack 25: More valuable than material things, one of the most precious gifts we can offer to others is our presence.

On our deathbed, confronted by the cold reality that our life is ending, material possessions, fame, power, looks, our university degrees and other concerns that used to consume us will all fade in importance. I learned this from dying patients who we interviewed for a research project. All of our research participants knew they were close to death and many of them talked about the importance of the gift of presence.

They felt the generosity of spirit of their doctor or nurse in the form of a felt presence. The subjects felt that, despite having hectic schedules, their clinicians were happy to see them, were sincere and were there for them. Generosity of spirit came in the form of a smile or sharing a joke.

One female participant said of her doctor: 'He is always happy to see you … he never acts as if there is anything else he needs to do, except see you.'

Another patient said, 'He is warm, his aura is really lovely, you know. He greets you with a smile every time and he will chuckle away.'

In giving the gift of presence, we give our total attention to the person we are with, as that person is the most important being in our life at that very moment.

Self-reflection

When your child talks about their day at school, are you generous with your presence and attention?

When your partner complains about their day, even when you're tired yourself, are you generous with your presence and attention?

How much genuine attention do you give to friends and colleagues who are in a pickle?

Would you rather terminate the exchange quickly as the situation becomes uncomfortable?

Initially, the gift of presence and acknowledgment can seem harder to give than material gifts. It requires a conscious intention to be present and an openness of heart to whatever may transpire. It is possible that the object of your acknowledgment might ignore or even reject your gift.

Despite the possible risk of rejection, the beauty of this type of generosity is that we can engage in it in countless moments, many times during the day. Gift of presence or acknowledgment can be as simple as genuinely recognising the waiter who brings you your food, or saying hello to the janitor. Engaging in small talk can be uplifting not just to the other person but to ourselves as well.

Many of us are hesitant to give money to beggars. Greeting them and even saying 'Have a good day' does not cost us materially in any form. Thanking people who allow us to merge on the motorway by giving them a wave is a small but generous act of acknowledgment of their kindness. Doing so also reinforces their generous behaviour.

As social creatures who desire and crave acknowledgment and attention, the gift of presence is life sustaining and reaffirming. Thích Nhất Hạnh said, 'Perhaps the greatest gift we can offer anyone is the gift of our full attention.'

Hack 26: Generosity can be in the form of acts of service, witnessed or hidden, with the goal of benefiting other beings.

Susan

Susan was in her last few months of life. She was in her sixties and had dealt with cancer for several years. The disease had spread to multiple parts of her body including her bones and brain.

She told me about an incident that occurred when she was admitted to the oncology ward at Auckland Hospital. She had had complications from chemotherapy and had to be rushed to the hospital. Once in the ward, she asked for a hat as she had no hair and was feeling cold. Her nurse told her that there were no more beanies or head coverings available.

A young Māori nurse overheard the discussion and, without saying anything, left the ward, went to her car – which was parked quite a distance from the hospital – and got her own beanie, which she handed to Susan when she returned. There were not many words exchanged.

As she recounted the story, Susan was in tears. That single act of service was the most memorable experience Susan had had during all her countless hospital stays.

Generous acts of service can be spontaneous and unplanned, such as the one the young nurse gave to Susan. In our day-to-day lives, small, conscious acts of generosity may come in the form of opening doors for other people or letting them get in the supermarket queue ahead of you. These acts of service can also be hidden so that no one will ever know about them, like picking up litter when you are at the beach or wiping the sink in an airline lavatory, so it is more presentable to the next passenger. These acts are not done automatically but instead are consciously planned, remembering that our covert action will benefit other beings.

Volunteering one's time on a regular basis to charitable organisations is an excellent way to be generous. Apart from the actual good the volunteering results in, committing to a regular time ensures that these generous acts are not dependent on our fluctuating mood, motivation, or whim.

Regardless of how I feel, I know that Wednesday mornings are devoted to running the meditation group at Lima Unit in Mount Eden Prison in Auckland. If I hadn't made a commitment, my hours at the prison would be erratic and this could disadvantage prisoners who might be looking forward to the sessions.

Building a regular generous act of service into one's weekly or monthly schedule makes these acts become part of our routine.

Levels of generosity

I asked a visiting Canadian monk if there are different types of generosity. Is there such a thing as bad generosity, where the act of generosity is performed with selfish motivation? For example, a politician who helped build an orphanage with the main intention being to promote himself for the next election.

The monk said that all forms of generosity are good, as they benefit other beings, however, he qualified that there are different levels of generosity.

When we give something that we really do not care for, say an old pair of jeans that have not seen the light of the day for 10 years, that type of generosity is called beggarly giving. It is giving things that are not worth our time anymore, sharing leftovers or scraps.

Another type of beggarly giving is when the giver is ambivalent about giving. 'Should I give or not? Probably, I might need it in the future ...' Both the receiver and the giver benefit to an extent, but not much, from this level of giving.

The second level of giving is friendly giving. This type of giving involves parting with things that we still value or enjoy. We part with the object (or time and service) willingly, spontaneously and with an open heart. We delight from this act of giving.

The third level of giving is regal giving. We offer the best that we have, what we treasure the most, with no reservation and with totally open arms, even if there is nothing left for ourselves. This is the pinnacle of giving. This is giving with deep wisdom. The mind is joyful.

When we look deeply at what we perceive as our possessions, we never actually own them. We were only temporary custodians of our belongings. Essentially, we own nothing. As we understand this truth, we realise there is no getting, possessing and giving.

CHAPTER 8

The benefits of generosity

One day back in 2014, I was between appointments and decided to while the time away by having a look around the supermarket. I really didn't need anything, so I just got a bottle of soft drink. As I queued to pay for it, the young father in front of me was having a discussion with the cashier. He was with three children, all under the age of about six, all barefoot and looking a bit bedraggled. His purchases were staples including nappies, toilet paper, butter, powdered milk, fresh milk, loaves of white bread, sausages, stewing beef and potatoes. All up, his bill was $126.56. He only had $100 with him, and he and the cashier were trying to work out which items he would need to return.

The fact he couldn't afford to pay for some of the necessities for his young family broke my heart. I spoke to the cashier and asked her to charge me for his whole bill. The young man initially refused but I was not going to allow him to forgo any of the basic items he needed. Outside the supermarket, he thanked me profusely and asked for my details so he could pay me back. I told him not to worry as I was also benefitting from helping him out.

The reason I remember all the items he bought was because I kept the receipt for that $126.56 in my wallet until it eventually disintegrated. Every time I looked at that receipt, I had a warm glow in my heart, a feeling that I could be of benefit to someone, a feeling that we are all in this together. That $126.56 spent brought me a lot of happiness. In fact, it was the best $126.56 spent of my life. That man benefited from my action, but I think that I benefited more than him. I still feel good every time I think about that supermarket incident and the receipt.

Hack 27: Give generously and you will feel better.

A group of scientists in Canada decided to find out whether spending money on others resulted in more happiness than spending money on themselves. To find out if this was true, they surveyed more than 600 Americans, asking them their annual income, their bills and expenses, gifts for themselves, gifts for others and donations to charities. They were also asked about their happiness. They found that how people spent their money was related to their happiness, and that spending money on others was a more effective route to happiness than spending money on oneself.

They did a follow-up study of 16 employees who received a profit-sharing bonus of about $5000. Their happiness scores were measured a month before their bonus and six to eight weeks after their bonus. Their spending was also measured. The researchers looked at their bills, expenses, spending on themselves and others, and donations to charities. Again, the scientists found that those who spent more on others experienced greater happiness.

However, the above studies are observational studies in which scientists make links or associations. Observational studies show that when we see A, we also see B. They do not show a cause-and-effect relationship, that A causes B.

A more powerful study is a causal study, where A is shown to cause B. Does spending money on others really result in happiness? The researchers pursued this question in their third study.

In this study, 46 participants rated their happiness in the morning. They were then given an envelope that contained either $5 or $20. They were asked to spend the money by 5pm that day. One group of participants was asked to spend the money on a bill, an expense, or a gift for themselves. The second group was asked to spend the money on a gift for someone else or a charitable organisation. At 5pm that day, they were asked to report their happiness scores. The study showed that participants who spent the money on others were significantly happier than those who spent the money on themselves.

The findings from these three research studies go against the western capitalist notion that accumulating wealth and money will make us happy. It appears that spending on others will make us happier.

. . . .

Hack 28: Giving generously makes you look attractive.

. . . .

The following comment from the Buddha sounds a bit dubious. He said that someone who gives gifts is 'handsome, comely, graceful, endowed with supreme beauty of complexion.' How can someone who gives gifts be perceived as beautiful?

In 2021, a study was published that showed that people who give are more likely to be perceived as good looking. Is it possible that someone who gives generously is so full of joy that they age slowly? Genuinely generous people often do not obsess on their own problems and instead focus on how to help other people, which results in them experiencing less stress. One other explanation is that when someone is perceived to be generous, that person is seen by others as a potential worthy partner or friend. Our brains might have evolved to notice and appreciate acts of generosity by others as generosity can help the species survive and propagate.

Hack 29: When you give generously, you receive generously.

The Buddha mentioned that what is given is not lost but is returned to the giver in some beneficial form, even in the form of wealth. It seems that when we give, we gain.

I know someone who has been focused on helping other people since her teenage years. She has unconditionally helped neighbours, friends, family, charities and religious organisations of various persuasions. She worked in the banking industry and even in that field, she organised for businesspeople to regularly donate to charities and help improve local communities.

What is remarkable is that the more she gave, the more she received. Her business grew but she kept her lifestyle and business operation low-key. Instead of renting a flash building in the business district to house her operations, she built a simple office in her home. Her staff were treated like family, to the extent that they regularly had lunches prepared by the woman's mother. She also helped her staff acquire their own properties and vehicles. Now that she is retired, she spends a lot of her spare time educating the urban poor in Manila to become financially literate. Despite having retired, she continues to engage in various business opportunities that bring her wealth.

It may seem trite, but I have a feeling that the Buddha is correct again when he said that when we give, we receive not just emotional points but materially as well.

Hack 30: Generous giving can result in peace and contentment.

From a worldly perspective, generous giving requires effort, results in diminution of resources and leads to a loss of one's time. From a giver's perspective, giving is costly from every angle. However, from my own experience and backed by research in neuroscience and psychology, the giver benefits in terms of experiencing the warm, emotional glow of giving, feeling purposeful and connected, looking attractive and feeling happy. How can you say no to that?

From a Buddhist perspective, generous giving chips away at what the Buddha says are the causes of our suffering — attachment, greed and a preoccupation with the self. When we give generously regularly, we cling less to money, possessions, time, rank, image and even our fixed opinions. We realise that we really do not own anything and that we are merely temporary custodians of whatever we have. Eventually, we let go of the things that control us. In liberation, we find peace and contentment. Generous giving is a strong foundation for a good and kind life.

· ·

Hack 31: Noticing acts of generosity around you can make you feel good.

· ·

In the last couple of centuries, our image as a species has been maligned. We, as humans, are described as selfish, short-sighted, destructive, cruel and extremely violent. Proof of this can be seen in world wars, the increasing gap between the haves and have nots, worsening climate change and the extinction of species brought on by relentless destruction of nature, which is often fuelled by greed.

Though there is some truth to these claims, humans are also capable of incredible ingenuity, creativity and unfathomable kindness and generosity. We really are not different from our siblings, the chimpanzees. Chimpanzees can be vicious and destructive, yet also caring and loving.

One aspect of our complex humanity that always pulls my heartstrings is when I witness generosity. It reminds me that humans have the capacity to be good. Observing acts of generosity and seeing how they benefit other people makes me teary and emotional (in a positive way).

I get my regular fix of it by watching acts of generosity on television, YouTube and Facebook. It is possible that some of the shows I watch may have been scripted, like *Undercover Boss,* in which top executives from successful companies pretend to be ordinary employees for a few days. The undercover boss invariably gets to find out about the lives and difficulties of their rank-and-file employees. The boss's relationships with their employees change and, not unusually, the boss's own life and relationships change. At the end of the show, the boss gives generously to the employee. These gifts can range from a small cash grant, to an opportunity for further training in the company, to holidays and even new homes.

Another reality TV show I was hooked on was *Secret Millionaire.* The plot is similar to *Undercover Boss,* but the wealthy people go and live in an impoverished neighbourhood for a week. They are given basic accommodation and a small budget for the week. Their goal is to become friendly with locals, get to know about the difficulties they experience in their lives and connect with local charities. At the end of the show, they donate a minimum of $100,000 to people or organisations in the community. Witnessing people's lives change as a result of someone's generosity is priceless and often a tearjerker for me. Not unexpectedly, the life of the giver also changes.

Lucky

I follow a young Filipino man named Lucky or 'kingLuckss' on social media. He is not a millionaire but might eventually become one given his millions of followers on both Facebook and YouTube. He goes out to the poor communities and takes on various personas to see how people will respond to him.

The benefits of generosity

Once he took on the role of a homeless beggar. He approached Bekbek, a woman selling turnips at a roadside stall. Lucky asked how much the turnips cost and Bekbek told him that a bunch cost about $1. Lucky said he had no money and asked if he could pay later.

Bekbek offered him a bunch of turnips for free. She then offered him a chair to sit on. Lucky learned that she had six children, and she had to sell turnips to survive. Her husband was unemployed and did occasional casual farm work. Sometimes, they just ate rice with onions and soy sauce, sweet potato leaves and vinegar, or fried fish.

After finding out about her life, Lucky returned the rest of the turnips Bekbek had given him, but she insisted that he take them. Lucky promised that when he eventually earned some money he would pay her back. She said there was no need, then told him that even if he was poor, as long as he helped others in need, everything would be okay.

Lucky then offered to pay her $50! She refused to take the money and said that he needed the money to get back to his hometown and buy food for himself. Lucky insisted she took the money, but she continued to refuse, saying he needed it more than she did. Bekbek then gave Lucky more turnips and her own lunch of bananas, crackers and sticky rice!

The clip ended with Lucky revealing that he was not poor and insisted on giving her $300, a huge amount of money equivalent to more than a month's salary in rural Philippines.

This clip is special not just because Lucky helped other poor Filipinos. What touched me the most was the natural capacity of a poverty-stricken turnip vendor to give generously, beyond her means to someone else in need. Witnessing acts of generosity, simulated or not, reminds me of the intrinsic goodness of humans.

Challenges to generosity

Angela

Greed causes more feeling of want and craving; generosity creates contentment and happiness.

Angela was known in her social circle as the ultimate taker. Once, she organised a party at her house, but she didn't prepare any food as she expected the visitors to bring food with them. At subsequent parties and get-togethers she attended, she never took anything to share. Instead, she would ask to take home leftover food.

Everyone was surprised when she arrived at another party with a big piece of good-quality ham. Everyone was stunned by her unexpected generosity. In the kitchen, she asked for an electric knife to cut the ham. Then she sliced the ham, put it into a container and took it home with her. She'd only brought it to the party so she could borrow the host's electric knife.

From the outside, her friends did not have much insight into her internal struggles, but Angela was not liked by her social group or her family. When her marriage dissolved in an acrimonious manner, her husband gave her all the matrimonial property, but it wasn't enough. She wanted more and sued for a proportion of his future income. No matter how much she had, she always wanted more. She remained unhappy, alone and was rarely invited out.

It appears that the more you take, the less you have. In a paradoxical way, focusing on accumulating results in feeling more lack.

Greed is a huge topic in Buddhism as it is one of the three poisons, along with hatred and ignorance. These three lead to suffering, dissatisfaction and unhappiness. In Buddhism, greed refers not only to desiring material objects like money or objects. Greed also refers to an unhealthy desire for sensual pleasures, mental states, future experiences, rank and power.

John D Rockefeller was an American industrialist, who at one point was the wealthiest American, if not the richest human alive at the time. Apparently, the story goes, he was asked how much money was enough money, and he replied, 'Just a little bit more.'

In an article in *The Atlantic* in 2011, Graeme Wood wrote about a Boston College study that asked a number of people whose annual income was over $25 million how much they would have to earn to feel they had enough. Most said they needed at least a quarter more than what they had. Of course, even if they got that, they would still think they needed a quarter more to be satisfied. Clearly, they would never be satisfied.

Humans are complex beings and all of us harbour various desires that can conflict with each other. We have an innate tendency to be kind and compassionate, but at the same time, we have evolved capacities to be vicious and greedy. Greed definitely had a role in our evolution, otherwise we wouldn't have varying degrees of it.

The problem with greed is that it is bottomless. Even if you have achieved your goal of saving a million dollars, if there is a smidgen of greed in your system, part of you will feel it is not enough.

Matthieu Ricard encapsulates greed concisely: 'Greed is the salty water consumed by those who thirst for self-centred gratification. This kind of thirst can never be quenched and becomes the source of increasing torment.'

I have known a few − but fortunately not that many − people who are seen as greedy. One common denominator for greedy people is a feeling of lack, that they are always missing something, and that what they have is not enough. Despite having what others will see as adequate or more than enough resources, internally they feel lacking. The issue is not necessarily the amount of wealth they have amassed, but a mental attitude that they are in scarcity, and if not now, they will be in the future.

One interesting Tibetan practice to encourage generosity is the practice of taking an object like a potato or a turnip and holding it in one hand then passing it into the other hand repeatedly until it becomes easy. Then the potato or turnip is switched for an object of more value, like rice, money or jewellery.

The giving from one hand to the other is a symbol for relinquishing or giving up. I am not sure how many greedy people would want to try the potato manoeuvre to enhance generosity.

The techniques used by shows like *Secret Millionaire* and *Undercover Boss* might be more feasible. Getting to know people who need help, viewing them as fellow humans and co-travellers in this life is achievable. Being familiar with the profound suffering of others, if the heart is open, is a catalyst for generosity. It is even possible that, once they are bitten by the generosity bug, previously greedy people might become genuine philanthropists.

Some people, who are not necessarily greedy, actively choose not to help others monetarily or materially. They have a perception that poor people will misuse the money given to them.

A common notion is that the money you give homeless people will be used to buy alcohol or drugs. This concern is understandable as it is not uncommon for homeless people to have problems with alcohol and drugs. This does not mean they cannot be shown generosity. They can be shown generosity by offering them food. Indirectly, one can be generous to organisations or charities that aim to eradicate homelessness. One can also choose to be generous, not just materially, but also by merely acknowledging their presence. A greeting of good morning, or a simple nod to say hello to acknowledge their existence and that you see them is a generous behaviour that might mean more to them than giving them a few coins.

Hack 32: Notice your mind and body before you give, when you give and after you give.

The act of giving is not as simple as just giving. When you decided to give $50 to a friend's fundraising campaign for child cancer, was it a genuine desire to help with child cancer or were there hidden hooks attached? These can be in the form of an expectation that your friend will also donate to your pet charity. Another hidden hook is the public acknowledgment that you will get when your name is posted on the donor list.

Self-reflection

When fundraising volunteers approach you for loose cash or coins, do you give because you really want to share some cheer? Or do you do it just to shut the person up because they have been a bit pushy?

Mindfulness or awareness of our mental state can help illuminate our motivations when we give or don't give.

How do you feel before making a donation?

Did it feel exciting, or did you feel coerced?

In the process of making a donation, how was your body?

How was your mind? Did it feel tight, or was there a release and relaxation?

After you made your donation, how did you feel?

Did you have a warm glow, or did you immediately check your bank account?

Being mindful of the act of giving can clarify whether our giving is beggarly, friendly or kingly/queenly. Without judgment, after realising our giving was beggarly, we can ask ourselves why it was so. If we notice that we felt tense, contracted and close-hearted, it might be because we gave too much. Sometimes, there is a feeling of guilt that we gave too little.

Being mindful of the process of giving might reveal that we have hooks and expectations from the recipient. Mindfulness in giving can help us understand our deep motivations, skilful or otherwise, which will allow us to work on them. Being mindful of genuine generous giving can make us realise how much the act of generous giving makes us feel meaningful, purposeful and connected to others. This then reinforces further generous giving.

Hack 33: A single act of generosity can reverberate and cause an impact beyond what we can imagine.

There is no question that both giver and receiver benefit from generosity. This is evidenced from the available scientific literature and from the personal experiences of givers and recipients of generous giving. But does it end there?

Apart from the direct recipient, do other people or beings benefit from single acts of generosity? Does generosity create a ripple effect that affects multiple individuals across time and space?

Mr Chan

Now in his late fifties, Mr Chan is a tour guide in Cambodia. In the small village where he grew up his father was a teacher and his mother owned a small store. He was the youngest of seven siblings. Today, he is the lone survivor of a massacre by Pol Pot in which his family was killed in the late 1970s. He is a licensed tour guide in Siem Reap, where the famous Angkor Wat can be found.

If called by the tourist agency to do some guiding, which happens a couple of times a week if he is lucky, he earns around $20 to $40 a week. A typical low-wage worker in

Cambodia earns about $50 a week. To supplement their meagre income, his wife sells vegetables in the local market.

Despite having three young children at school and being in a very tight financial situation, Mr Chan is happy and content. He is thankful for whatever blessings come his way.

A few years ago, he guided two friends, Bill and Rich, for three days in a row. Before they said their goodbyes, Bill and Rich thanked him profusely for such an amazing guiding experience. In addition to his $40 guiding fee, they gave him a $60 tip.

He was so grateful and told them that it would allow him to buy some more flip flops. Curious, they asked him what he meant by getting more flip flops. Mr Chan told them that when he earned any more than $40 in a week, the rest of the money went towards buying flip flops. Then, on weekends, he drove out to remote villages to distribute the footwear to barefoot Cambodian kids.

Bill and Rich's curiosity was piqued. Bill asked if they could join him in his little mission. They went to the market where Mr Chan bought 20 pairs of children's flip flops in varying designs and colours.

Bill and Rich couldn't help but think of the hundreds if not thousands of shoeless children in remote villages. Footwear is a necessity in the tropics as it protects the feet not just from the hot ground but also from broken glass, sharp rocks and soil-based parasitic worms. Bill and Rich called a few of their friends from the US and they fundraised to buy as many sets of footwear as they could before they left the country.

Bill met Mr Chan before he and Rich left Cambodia and told him about their quick fundraising effort. The amount collected allowed Mr Chan to buy several hundred pairs of flip flops and shoes.

After they left Cambodia, Mr Chan sent Bill and Rich pictures of the carload of footwear he had bought. Later that week, he sent them pictures of the many children showing off their new footwear. It did not end there.

A couple of the children in the pictures had deformed toes. Bill became anxious as it reminded him of an infectious disease he had learned about in medical school. He asked Mr Chan to take close-up photographs of the afflicted children's feet and toes. He then asked permission from Mr Chan to show the pictures to his medical colleagues in the US.

His worst fears were realised. These children were suffering from leprosy. Before seeing those pictures, Bill had the misconception that leprosy had been eradicated.

Bill went on to coordinate with Mr Chan to ensure that the local health authorities were informed and that the children and their families were assessed and treated.

Our acts of generosity are like lighting a candle in a dark room. The flame of that single candle lights other candles, and then other candles, all of which brightly illuminate the once-dark room. Generosity causes a ripple effect that goes beyond what we can imagine. It is said that a small act of giving has repercussions in an interdependent and interconnected world. One small act of charity is said to be equal to countless acts of charity.

CHAPTER 9

Mindfulness

What the heck is mindfulness? It is a state of mind that is present, aware and at peace.

Mindfulness has various definitions and, despite the word's frequent use, there doesn't seem to be clear consensus among academics and Buddhist meditation masters regarding an English definition. I humbly offer my take on mindfulness: I define it as a state of mind that is aware, alert, noticing and kindly accepting of the moment-by-moment experience of the mind and the body, leading to kindness and compassion.

Billy

Around 2004, when I was a freshly minted psychiatrist, I had a very challenging patient in Auckland. Billy was one of two boys from a wealthy family. As the result of an accident when he was five years old, Billy walked with a noticeable limp.

As a young man in his early twenties, he was self-conscious about his limp and felt that no woman would ever be interested in him. Almost every Friday and Saturday night, he went clubbing and tried to meet women. He was unsuccessful in his pursuits and would come home drunk and dejected. His feelings of unlikability and ruminations on being a single man for the rest of his life peaked on Sunday evenings. His only relief was to superficially cut his inner thighs with a hunting knife.

It was common for me to see Billy – and his parents – for urgent assessments on Monday mornings. Our team tried various therapies, both medical and psychological, but Billy continued with his self-loathing and self-harming behaviours. Seeing Billy and his parents miserable and helpless on Monday mornings almost became routine for me. His parents even promised to build a new hospital if we could help their son.

Unusually for me, I went on leave for two months as I wanted to attend several overseas medical conferences. On my return, I was expecting to see the names of Billy and his parents on my patient list – but they weren't there. I didn't pay much attention to it on my first week back, but the following Monday, Billy's name was again not on my list. After a month of not seeing Billy, I started to worry. Had he accidentally cut his femoral artery? Was he dead? How come his nurse had not told me anything?

Filled with anxiety, I asked Billy's nurse how he had been. The nurse nonchalantly said, 'He's okay.'

I was stunned. How could he be okay? Was he okay in the psychiatric ward or the surgical ward? How could he be okay when nothing had worked for the past year?

The nurse told me that Billy had been doing well since he'd started a therapy course that involved mindfulness. That was my first encounter with mindfulness.

I had a couple of other patients, one with anxiety and the other with self-harm behaviours, attend the same course that Billy had attended and both of them benefited hugely from it.

I didn't know much about mindfulness as a psychological therapy, but I was intrigued. If three of my very unwell patients had benefited from it, I was sure it would help my own overthinking mind too.

I attended my first course on mindfulness at the Auckland Buddhist Centre. The course consisted of six two-hour evenings that involved short lectures and meditation practice.

Mindfulness as a psychological paradigm was very different from traditional western therapies like cognitive behavioural therapy or psychodynamic therapy. After six weeks of attending the course, I didn't notice any change in me. I was still the same old neurotic Tony. I trusted in the process though, as it had been around for 2600 years. That's 2500 years more than Freud, so there must be something in it!

I knew I had to be patient. I continued with mindfulness meditation practice almost daily, for around 15 minutes per session, for the next few months. I viewed it as mind fitness, not so different from going to the gym.

Around three months after I started the course, while driving down the motorway, a car cut me off without indicating, almost causing a crash. I observed the whole incident calmly and even wished that the other driver reached his destination safely.

Now, that was not the usual Tony. In the past, I would have got very angry, scowled at the other driver and wished them a long stay somewhere hot and flaming. Not this time, though. I think mindfulness practice has rewired a part of my brain.

Current fashion

Fast forward almost two decades and just about anywhere you go in the western world, you will find courses advertising mindfulness. There are countless apps and programmes offering lessons on mindfulness for stress relief, parenting, care of pets, sports coaching, insomnia, golf, toddlers and even the military. I've even briefly acted as an informal supervisor on a research project teaching mindfulness in the New Zealand Defence Forces.

Mindfulness is such a commonly used word that it has become synonymous with stress relief and relaxation. But is that what mindfulness really is?

Mindfulness can help with relaxation, but that is like using a Ferrari to drive to the supermarket two blocks down the road. Mindfulness is much more, much, much, much more than just feeling relaxed.

Some traditional meditation teachers have been alarmed by the extent of the commercialisation and bastardisation of mindfulness, as it has strayed far from what the Buddha taught about it. But Buddhists being Buddhists, they do not care much about Buddhist intellectual property rights. Some teachers even say that a little bit of mindfulness, even if it's not exactly what the Buddha taught, is better than no mindfulness at all.

Why the need for mindfulness?

Humans have evolved through natural selection to make sure we survive and pass on our genes to the next generation. To ensure that we survive, our brains are equipped with both the thinking mind and emotions.

The thinking mind can plan, strategise, predict the future and reflect on the past. The thinking mind allowed humans to observe nature and learn that certain plant species could be propagated and farmed. The thinking mind has realised that after so many moons, seasons will change and food will become scarce. Thinking humans then developed ways to preserve and store food. In our generation, the thinking mind has developed spacecraft that can cross the solar system and technology to identify viruses that cause pandemics.

We are also equipped with emotions, which provide rapid responses to our thoughts and surroundings in order to ensure our survival. When we see a tiger, the body and mind tell us – without thinking – that we should run. If someone attacks us – without thinking – we fight back. If a loved one dies, we signal to others – without thinking – through our tears and sadness that we need support and consolation.

Despite our frail, soft and vulnerable bodies, there is no doubt that evolution has gifted us with these two mechanisms, which allowed us to become the apex species on the planet. Though these two mechanisms allowed us to survive for 300,000 years, our thinking mind and emotions have also been the cause of much suffering. For many of us, our thinking mind and emotions can be out of control. Mindfulness allows us to notice the chaos, and in the noticing, we can do something about it.

Self-reflection

How many times have you become anxious over something that you later realise you need not have worried about?

How many times have you sent a message to a loved one only to see that they have read the message, but haven't replied?

What goes on in your mind when that happens?

If the message was to someone you'd just started dating, did you think that the other person might be losing interest in you? Did you think that they might have met someone else?

If the message was for your teenage child, did you think they might have been in an accident?

Mixed with the overthinking come the accompanying sore stomach, headache and difficulty breathing – all part of anxious emotions.

Papañca

Despite our best efforts, it's rare for us to have long periods of peace and tranquillity in our lives. Even if you are in a beautiful, peaceful setting, say walking calmly on the beach at sunset with not many people around, the smell of the ocean refreshing the soul, the warm, soft sand gently kissing your feet, the sound of seagulls in the distance ... then a childhood memory comes back of your father whacking you for giving chips to the seagulls when you were eight years old. This brief flashback brings on other thoughts. Now you think of how unlucky you were to have a father like him, that you could have excelled in life if you hadn't had such an awful father. Then your mind shifts to other matters that annoy you. 'Oh yeah, I have to pick up my son for football practice. He is always late. So annoying. And his mother will have forgotten about practice. My family is hopeless!'

Remember papañca?

Robbie

Robbie is a happily married man in his early thirties. After a delicious home-cooked meal, Robbie and his wife, Rebecca, settle snuggly on the couch to watch TV. Robbie reckons he must be the luckiest man alive.

During a commercial break, Rebecca reminds Robbie to empty the dishwasher. The *dishwasher*. Robbie's mind goes into overdrive.

She always has this thing about dishwashers. She wants them emptied right away. She has this scrupulous system where knives and forks must point downwards, bowls have to be turned towards the centre and plates arranged from large to small. She goes ballistic even with the slightest hint of over stacking.

Why can't he just do it his way? She never listens to him. Why has he ended up with this control freak? He should have gone out with Linda instead. She was way more relaxed and chilled. He hates his marriage. Maybe divorce is an option, but he doesn't want to lose the house. He might become homeless …

Robbie has just experienced a classic papañca. Just one stimulus, in his case, the word 'dishwasher' triggered an emotional tornado. Two minutes ago, before the trigger word dishwasher, Robbie had been the happiest man alive. Now, he was pondering divorce and homelessness.

Papañca is a word used in the Buddhist scriptures to refer to a mind that goes out of control, dredging past stories, weaving complex narrative twists and unlikely scenarios. The mind links other memories, thoughts, conversations, opinions, fears and frustrations seamlessly, which creates a tapestry of feeling and emotions often unrelated to what the person was experiencing before the trigger.

Papañca also refers to conceptual proliferation. It has an obsessive, unending and repetitive nature, which often results in mental tension and suffering. It often causes the mind to narrow its focus and forget the big picture. Without mindfulness, we tend to hop on a papañca express train without even knowing it.

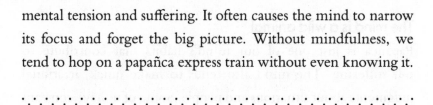

Hack 34: Know the trigger for your papañca. Is it from an external stimulus or from your own mind?

I had a medical colleague who was involved in an acrimonious legal battle against the hospital she worked for. Because of her open criticism of the hospital's inefficiencies and discriminatory policies, she was bullied by management. She ended up suing the hospital. The negotiations and hearings took a couple of years.

During those two years, every time she opened her email and saw the name of the hospital or her lawyer's name in her inbox, her mind went into overdrive, thinking of the worst-case scenarios, including losing her job and a counter-lawsuit from the hospital. It reached a point that just the thought of opening her emails brought on papañca.

Self-reflection

What are triggers for your papañca?

Is it a certain way your other half looks at you?

Is it seeing people from a certain demographic?

Is it certain movies or scenes in a TV show?

Is it food, a scent or physical sensation?

The mind is a wild animal

Papañca is just one of our mind's habits that contribute to our suffering. The mind also tends to make quick, irrational judgments about situations and people. Some of us have constant inner dialogues that tell us that we are not good enough despite all evidence to the contrary. Many of us demand instant gratification when a little bit of delay is not unreasonable. All of us have multiple cognitive biases and distortions, which often lead us to have unrealistic perceptions of the world.

The uncontrolled mind, with its reckless and unrestrained nature, its restlessness and irrationality, is often the cause of our suffering. One of my colleagues told me that her emotions constantly bullied her.

In the Buddhist scriptures, the mind has been described as a wild animal that is out of control. Since this out-of-control nature of the mind causes our immense pain and misery, it needs to be tamed.

Hack 35: When caught in a papañca, notice it and shift to a mindful mode.

The Buddha compares the process of training the mind to the taming of a wild animal. Just as an animal trainer needs to use various techniques to bring the animal under control, the meditator has to draw upon various methods to subdue the mind. Of the various mental techniques available to train the mind, the Buddha told his followers to keep mindfulness in the forefront of their minds. Mindfulness is a recognised antidote for a restless mind, a mind swimming in papañca.

Mindfulness allows us to see our experiences clearly. If Robbie had been mindful, he would have noticed his papañca being triggered by the word dishwasher. He would have noticed that his thoughts of divorce and homelessness were just empty thoughts that came and went.

When in a mindful mode, we can see our irrational thought patterns, emotional reactions, uncontrolled cravings and our desire for things to be different as random, ever changing and impermanent. We see them as reactive brain impulses. We have a choice to just let them pass or invest unnecessary energy in a never-ending rabbit hole of exhausting mental processes.

· ·

Hack 36: Mindfulness is one of the best ways to unhook ourselves from the click-baiting mind.

· ·

Mindfulness is a superpower because we see everything in our mind arise and pass away. Our thoughts are empty, like soap bubbles that come and go. Yet we still tend to engage with our crazy thoughts and emotions.

The mind sometimes behaves like a deceptive online seller. It employs exaggerated headlines or flashy advertisements that lure customers to its online stores and plays on the customers' fantasies or anxieties, which are often useless or lacking in substance. The mind wants us to click on its various attention-grabbing links. With mindfulness, you are aware that the eye-catching advertisements are there. They look enticing but you know that once you click, you are hooked. Or worse, scammed!

If I am being mindful at this very moment, I observe that I am staring at the laptop screen, noticing my fingers tapping away with a muted clickety clacking of the keys; hearing the amorphous background café music melding with soft conversations of customers; I am smelling the soft scent of some air deodoriser; feeling the pressure of the rolled-up towel on my butt to prop me up on the chair. I am noticing the sleeves of my jacket brushing on my wrist. A WhatsApp notification pinging. My mind is calm.

If I am not mindful, my mind will wander. That man eating his muesli is slurping ... how uncivilised. I cannot believe he was allowed to enter this posh café. Instead of writing, I should be hitting the pool and burning calories because my GP said my blood sugar is a bit high and is prediabetic. Yes, prediabetic! If I don't lose weight and improve my laboratory numbers, in a few years I will be taking insulin, going blind, losing the feeling in my feet, which will cause nasty infections. Maybe they'll have to be amputated ... That will ruin my swimming. Life is hard. Bloody hell, another message from the clinic! What is it this time?

Mindfulness and meditation

To many people in the west, mindfulness has become synonymous with the word meditation. Meditation is a general term that involves mental practices that result in various mind states including enhanced attention, increased insight, relaxation, stress relief and even sleep.

There are plenty of other types of meditation practice, both Buddhist and non-Buddhist, but here I will focus on mindfulness meditation. This is a specific form of meditation developed by the Buddha, and it is the best way to become mindful.

Six-piece musical band

Mindfulness is noticing the *moment-by-moment experience of the mind and the body.* That sounds complicated, doesn't it? What does moment-by-moment experience of the mind and body really mean? For me, this part of the mindfulness definition is best felt rather than explained. You might have gathered already that Buddhism emphasises experiential learning rather than intellectual or philosophical knowledge.

We can subdivide our moment-by-moment experience by what our various sense organs are registering. In Buddhist psychology, we have six senses, which include the traditional five senses of sight, hearing, smell, taste and touch. The sixth sense is the mind, which involves our thoughts, feelings and emotions.

A simple way of conceptualising our conscious moment-by-moment experience of the six sense organs is to imagine our awareness as a stage with six musical performers. This metaphor is derived from American Buddhist teacher Joseph Goldstein's concept of a 6-piece chamber orchestra. On the stage of our awareness are six performers: a vocalist who represents thoughts and emotions; a drummer who symbolises the sensations in the body; a lead guitarist who represents sight; a bass guitarist who represents hearing; a violinist who represents taste and a flautist who represents smell.

If this line-up isn't to your musical taste, you can assign the different sense organs to whatever musical performer you prefer.

At any one point, these six players are on our stage of awareness. For most of us, the vocalist, who represents thinking and emotions, tends to be the loudest. For the anxious and overthinking people like me, the vocalist takes control of the stage, with the rest of the players in the background.

If I have a stomach ache, the drummer, who represents the body, becomes loudest, with the vocalist singing various scary tunes like, 'It might be cancer!'

If I am focused on my food, the violinist (taste), lead guitar (sight) and flautist (smell) take centre stage. If I'm judging the food negatively and getting annoyed by the whole experience, the vocalist takes centre stage again: 'This is not nice, why are they feeding you this?'

When I am quietly mindfully meditating, fully absorbed by the breath, the drummer (body sensations) takes centre stage in a calm way, while the rest of the musicians are quiet. When my cell phone rings, the bass guitar (hearing) is triggered, followed by the vocalist (thoughts): 'Who is ringing me now? I am supposed to be meditating!'

When we are mindful, we are aware and watching what is going on in our moment-by-moment experience. We are alert and not sleepy. We notice the different things going on with the musicians. We are kind to them even if they are unruly and out of control at times.

Sometimes, when mindfulness is strong, we see the gaps between the music. We notice space. We eventually see the stage where all the happenings occur. This suggests that our ability to be aware is getting stronger.

Let's practise

Try the following short exercise to focus on your moment-by-moment mind and body experience.

Notice what is going on with the various musicians in your awareness.

Avoid adding stories or commentaries. Just focus on what you notice.

Pay full attention to what you are seeing.

Avoid making comments on what you see. Just see for a few seconds. Just *see*.

Pay attention to what are you hearing. Just hear for a few seconds. Just *hear*. If it is quiet, just notice the quiet.

Pay attention to your sense of smell. Just smell for a few seconds. Just *smell*. If there is no smell, notice there is no smell.

Pay attention to your sense of taste. Just taste for a few seconds. Just *taste*. If you cannot taste anything, note the absence of taste.

Pay attention to your body. Notice body sensations, the expansion and relaxation of your chest and abdomen while breathing, your clothes caressing your body, your buttocks pressing on the chair, your feet on the ground. Just *feel*.

Pay attention to your mind. What are you thinking about? What are your emotions like? Are you calm? Are you annoyed? Are you excited to be learning something new? Notice for a few seconds.

Congratulations! You just engaged in a mindfulness meditation practice.

If you didn't complete the exercise, notice what you are feeling now. Be aware of your thoughts about why you skipped the instructions. Did you feel bored? If you noticed boredom or sleepiness, that's being mindful as well. If you noticed that your mind was elsewhere, the fact that you became aware that you were thinking about something else is being mindful too.

Mindfulness is knowing the various characters in your mind.

Expanding the practice

Noticing our experience is an important aspect of mindfulness but it is not enough on its own. Remember the definition of mindfulness is a state of mind that is:

- aware and alert
- kind acceptance of moment-by-moment experiences
- leading to kindness and compassion.

Aware and alert

Our quality of noticing is important. We need to be *aware* and *alert*. Are we watching with alertness and relaxed vigilance? Or are we watching with dullness, not fully attentive to the experience? The other extreme is to watch with tension and hypervigilance. Like a stringed instrument, mindfulness has to be tuned just right. If the strings are too lax, the instrument will not sing. If the strings are too tight, they will snap.

Kind acceptance of moment-by-moment experiences

The next component of a mindful practice involves our attitude to our experience. A mindful attitude is peaceful and *kindly accepting of the experience*. Since whatever is going on at this specific moment is a culmination of multiple causes and conditions, many of which we do not have control over, we cannot do much to change the current situation at this very second. Instead, we have to accept it.

Acceptance, however, does not mean resignation that we cannot do anything about the future. An important aspect of mindfulness is knowing that what we do now, in speech or action, will influence the future. Accepting with kindness is vital in practising mindfulness because when we are kind to the situation, there is an attitude of peace and relaxation to whatever is happening.

I was once flying to London from New Zealand via Los Angeles. The airport in Los Angeles is notorious for having long queues and airport staff who have a penchant for screaming at airline passengers. I had a three-hour layover there, which is tight at the best of times. Our plane arrived an hour late, which meant that my layover was down to two hours.

I was at the back of the plane, so it took a while for me to disembark. As I waited, a sense of dread overcame me, a pit in my stomach, cold clammy hands, throbbing headache, and tightened breathing. My mind went into overdrive. If I missed my connection, I'd have to deal with long queues at the transfer desk, then I'd have to tell the conference organisers in London that I might not make it to my talk. I worried that this might tarnish my professional reputation and people would think I was unreliable.

Then I had a mindful moment, and I noticed that I was close to panic. I consciously watched my breathing, noticed my body tension, noticed the anxious mind. It was pointless getting mad at the airlines or the airport.

The plane being late was a result of multiple variables including a slight delay departing Auckland because of a sick passenger, strong headwinds and the busy air traffic in LA's airspace. I had a choice to be angry and tense, or to kindly accept that this was the current situation from which I could not escape.

I chose the latter and I noticed my chest relax, my back loosen and my breathing ease. I calmly made a contingency plan, which included calling my travel agent to get help organising an alternate connecting flight if I needed it. I called the conference organisers to let them know I might be delayed. I asked airport staff if I could get ahead of the immigration queue in order to make my flight. Surprisingly, I was calm throughout the process. Eventually, I made my flight to London on time, so all that worrying and papañca was not worth it!

Leading to kindness and compassion

The last component of the mindfulness definition is often neglected in western interpretations. In many western and modern definitions, mindfulness is limited to awareness and concentration training without any reference to ethical behaviour.

As such, a sniper could develop high levels of awareness, alertness and focus, which makes him 'mindful' and an efficient killing machine. This is totally against the Buddhist definition of mindfulness where 'with mindfulness as his gatekeeper, the noble disciple abandons the unwholesome and develops the wholesome ...'

According to Ajahn Amaro, if so-called mindfulness practice does not involve ethical sensitivity, it cannot be said to be genuine mindfulness.

An important aspect of daily mindfulness practice is cultivating wholesome, kind, generous, compassionate thoughts and actions, while abandoning harmful, hateful and greedy tendencies.

What mindfulness is not

Mindfulness is not religious

Even though mindfulness was developed by the Buddha, it is compatible with any other religion or philosophical movement. The whole practice and philosophy does not concern itself with the afterlife, the spirit world, gods and deities. I often tell students in my meditation classes that mindfulness, if practised regularly, will make them better Christians, Muslims, Jews, Hindus, Jains, Sikhs, agnostics or atheists.

Joan

Joan was a patient of mine with significant anxiety. She constantly worried about the future. What would happen to her children? Would her husband leave her? Would she be around to see her children get married? Despite her significant anxiety, she refused to engage in cognitive behavioural therapy. She was loath to try medications.

Since there was growing evidence in the scientific domain regarding the effectiveness of mindfulness in anxiety, I suggested that she consider it. I told her about the principles and the increasing evidence of its usefulness, and she was receptive to it. I provided her with some basic literature, websites and names of apps for her to check out.

At our follow-up visit, she said she could not practise mindfulness because, according to her pastor, it came from the Buddha and anything non-Christian was from the devil.

I was a bit stunned by her pastor's extremist viewpoint. I explained to her that it was true that mindfulness practice was developed by the Buddha, but the actual practice did not concern itself with life after death, with God or with anything spirit related. I even told her that there were Christian variations of mindfulness that used words and phrases from the Bible as mantras. The pastor won and my patient left with untreated anxiety.

Mindfulness is not emptying the mind

A common misconception regarding mindfulness meditation is that it involves emptying the mind or stopping the mind from its inner chatter. In fact, some of my students complain, after the first five minutes of meditation, that they cannot practise mindfulness meditation because their minds are too busy, and they cannot stop their thinking. The more they try to stop thinking, the more their mind ties itself into knots. I remind them that our minds have evolved to constantly think and feel. That's the mind's purpose. Telling someone to stop thinking is like telling them to stop breathing.

In the practice of mindfulness, one observes what goes on in the mind and the body. The observation is calmly undertaken and if it sees the mind as busy and frenetic, then one notices with acceptance that the mind is busy and frenetic. If the practitioner does not complicate the situation by adding an extra inner dialogue like 'I am such a failure, I cannot even freaking stop my mind from thinking', eventually the mind settles and slows down.

The fact that the practitioner notices that the mind is busy is already being mindful!

After some experience with the practice, there will be brief periods of space and stillness. However, to expect the mind to stop thinking in the beginning of the practice is unrealistic. It is like expecting to do a marathon after your first running session.

Be patient; it takes a few weeks or even months to become comfortable with mindfulness. In my own experience, I became comfortable with it after attending a three-day mindfulness retreat.

. . . .

Hack 37: Being mindful is not having expectations during the mindfulness exercise.

. . . .

Mindfulness is more than stress relief

Mindfulness often can result in temporarily feeling calm and relaxed. Even for beginners, particularly if they engage in mindfulness of the breath, the breath has a natural calming effect. In fact, even without mindfulness instructions, just watching your breath arise and pass can result in stress relief.

However, to define mindfulness as simply stress relief is like eating in a Michelin-star restaurant and saying you just had a feed. Mindfulness is much more than just feeling some calm and stress relief. Though mindfulness can result in stress relief, the rationale for mindfulness practice is to be acquainted with mind patterns that cause suffering so that you can do something about that suffering.

There will be times when the mindfulness practice does not result in calm, especially if you are experiencing difficult emotions. It does not mean that your meditation practice was a failure. Paradoxically, wanting your anger or irritation to disappear by doing mindfulness practice is not being mindful at all. It might even make your emotions more intense.

Remember, mindfulness is calmly accepting the current situation. It is in the process of acceptance that peace and relaxation can occur. If you have persevered in watching difficult thought patterns and tough emotions during the practice, you have done a great job. Be careful not to expect to feel calm and relaxed as a result of the meditation.

Does it really work?

Mindfulness first appeared in the scientific literature in 1966, followed by a couple of publications in 1979 and 1982. It was the third mindfulness publication in 1982, a study on the effectiveness of mindfulness in chronic pain by Jon Kabat-Zinn, that brought mindfulness into the realm of western psychology and medicine. Kabat-Zinn made mindfulness, a Buddhist meditation practice, acceptable and normalised in the western world.

Since then, the research on mindfulness has grown exponentially, with more than 16,000 scientific papers published by 2021. Most of the studies I am about to quote from are review papers rather than individual research studies. Review papers endeavour to analyse the results of multiple studies and attempt to come up with conclusions based on several – often conflicting – research results.

In a review publication consisting of 14 combined studies, mindfulness has been shown to be effective in helping many conditions including reducing stress, depression, anxiety and distress among healthy subjects.

In a separate study of patients with psychiatric disorders, S. B. Goldberg and his group analysed 142 clinical trials consisting of 12,005 patients. They found that mindfulness-based interventions helped with depression, pain, smoking and addictions among those with psychiatric diagnosis.

There are also strong suggestions that mindfulness benefits those with physical illnesses, at least in their ability to manage distress and disability in everyday life.

With all of the documented benefits of mindfulness for psychological and physical health, I am not surprised that mindfulness has also been shown to change brain activity and structure. Mindfulness enhances attention to the present moment, so the anterior cingulate cortex, a brain region associated with attention, changes in activity and structure with mindfulness practice.

Mindfulness has also been demonstrated to help practitioners regulate their emotions. Brain regions involved in emotional regulation like the fronto-limbic area are shown to be enhanced during mindfulness practice.

A common tendency of humans is to 'mind wander' or become lost in thoughts. Getting lost in thoughts, which usually involve ruminating about the past, worrying about the future or events that most likely will not happen at all, has been associated with unhappiness. The brain region implicated in this process is the default mode network. Several research studies show that mindfulness practice dampens down the activity in this network following mindfulness training compared to control subjects. One can then extrapolate that with mindfulness practice, the mind is more attentive to the present, which is linked to being happier.

Does mindfulness make us more youthful? When you meet Buddhist monks and nuns, guessing their ages is often a fraught activity. Most of the time, one underestimates their age, as they look younger than their chronological age. It could be the bald head, the robes or the jolly demeanour that makes us think they are younger. Many monks and nuns from Thailand also shave their eyebrows, which makes speculating their age more difficult. However, there might be some biological basis as to why Buddhist monks and nuns who regularly meditate appear younger than their real age.

Telomeres are caps at the tip of chromosomes, and telomere length is used as an indicator of cellular aging. Shorter telomeres suggest worsening health and early death, while longer telomeres suggest youthfulness and robust health. There have been studies looking at the relationship between mindfulness and telomere length. A review paper that combined 11 studies showed that individuals who practised mindfulness meditation had longer telomeres than the control group. Also, those who meditated longer seemed to see greater effects on telomere length.

In summary, rigorous scientific work shows that mindfulness can be beneficial in terms of the psychological and physical health of practitioners. The mindful mind is less likely to wander into dark ruminations or scary projections into the future, which are associated with unhappiness. Lastly, mindfulness practitioners might live longer lives.

The research on mindfulness has exploded to the point that, at one neuroscience conference I attended a decade ago, even the Dalai Lama suggested that we should stop studying mindfulness as there is already extensive research data showing that it is clearly helpful for the human condition. He exhorted the hundreds of mindfulness researchers at that meeting to shift their focus from researching mindfulness to teaching and practising mindfulness daily.

CHAPTER 10

How to develop mindfulness

The best way to develop mindfulness is through mindfulness meditation. You can read as much as you want about mindfulness, but just having knowledge will not make you mindful. The process of developing mindfulness is no different from learning a new sport or a musical instrument. Reading or watching videos about them just increases your theoretical knowledge but will not translate into making you a better sportsperson or musician.

Mindfulness meditation allows us to dive into our moment-by-moment experience and apply the principles of alertness and peaceful acceptance. With regular practice, it is possible for each of us to have a mindful attitude daily, or even on a moment-by-moment basis.

There are various types of mindfulness meditation practice, including mindfulness of the breath, the body, feelings and mind. However, most people find that mindfulness of breathing is the most accessible and doable. In fact, mindfulness of breathing was the main meditation style that the Buddha himself used.

Mindfulness of the breath

The Buddha gave specific, detailed instructions on mindfulness. Here is a short excerpt of his words:

> *Here a monk, gone to the forest, to the foot of a tree, or to an empty hut, sits down; having folded his legs crosswise, straightened his body, and established mindfulness in front of him, just mindful he breathes in, mindful he breathes out. Breathing in long, he understands: 'I breathe in long'; or breathing out long, he understands: 'I breathe out long'. Breathing in short, he understands: 'I breathe in short'; breathing out short, he understands: 'I breathe out short'.*

In mindfulness of the breath practice, the main object we focus on is the breath. We watch attentively as the breath does its natural process of rising and passing. When we get distracted, we notice we get distracted, without judgment, and return again to the breath.

The practitioner is instructed to be in a quiet place so there will be the least amount of distraction. In the beginning, a quiet environment is conducive to mind training. However, once a practitioner is more experienced, they can do mindfulness practices in noisy and busy places.

Practise mindfulness of the breath

1. Sit down comfortably on a chair or a cushion.

We often associate meditation practices with sitting in a lotus position on a cushion or even the floor. This is not necessary. The important thing is that you are comfortable, have a stable posture and can sustain the position for the duration of the meditation practice.

2. While seated, your back should be straight to promote alertness of the mind.
An alert mind is important in this practice as we are training our awareness and not promoting dullness or sleepiness. Avoid being stiff; a stiff back causes tension in the mind.

3. Close your eyes, as visual stimulation can be distracting.
If you find closing your eyes feels threatening or you think you might fall asleep, leave them half open, focused loosely on the floor about a metre or two away from you.

4. Place your hands where they feel comfortable.
If I am on a chair, I rest my hand on my knees. If I am on a cushion, my right hand is over the left, resting comfortably near my belly button.

5. Before you start the meditation, try putting a half-smile on your face.
Meditation should not be stressful or tense. We are trying to train a peaceful and happy mind. Putting on a half-smile lightens the burden and eases the tension we hold in our body.

6. Once comfortably seated, take a few deep, slow breaths to acquaint yourself with the feeling of breathing.

7. After a few deep breaths, breathe normally.
Try not to control the breath. Watch the breath as if you are watching waves on a beach come and go. Waves come and go. The breaths just come and go.

8. Pay attention to the sensation of breathing.
Notice the feeling of breathing in the body, the movement of air through the nose to the chest, the expansion and relaxation of the chest and abdomen, and the release of the breath. With full but relaxed attention, you will become intimately aware of breathing.

You will be distracted

Even after a few breath cycles, you will get distracted. Thoughts like 'This is stupid, I should be doing something else' or 'I am such a loser, I cannot even focus on this simple breath' are common. Many beginner meditators daydream, forgetting that the task is to pay attention to the breath. We also get distracted by emotions like being annoyed or bored. Another distraction is an urge to move or scratch. These are all common experiences, and the best approach is to peacefully acknowledge the distraction.

Once you realise that you are distracted by thoughts, emotions, urges or physical discomfort, that is an incredible moment of *awareness*. This is what we are trying to develop in mindfulness. Throughout the day, many of us are blindly unaware of what our minds are doing, as we are often lost in our thoughts and emotions.

When you become aware that you are distracted while meditating, acknowledge *kindly* that you got distracted, and without fuss, return your attention to the breath.

Be careful about the self-critical mind if it tells you that you are not really the meditating type. It is just a thought, a distraction, a mind bubble that can be let go.

If you get distracted 99 times in a five-minute practice, but realise that you got distracted 99 times, those are 99 examples of awareness training and you are already achieving what we are training for in a mindfulness meditation practice.

Remember the definition of mindfulness. It is a state of mind that is *aware, alert, noticing and kindly accepting of moment-by-moment experiences of the mind and the body.*

We become aware that we got side-tracked. We kindly accept our experience, without judgment or self-criticism. Once we become aware of the distraction, we return our attention to the breath.

· ·

Hack 38: Counting, noting and using phrases can help the distracted mind in mindfulness meditation.

· ·

There are various strategies you can use to help focus the mind on the breath. These techniques are helpful not just for beginner meditators. If my mind is particularly busy and is constantly distracted, I use techniques like counting, noting or using phrases.

Please use counting, noting or using phrases as a beginner or when your mind is particularly distracted or busy. They are helpful tools for focusing and training in attention.

Counting

Counting the breath is an age-old strategy to focus a distracted mind.

After breathing in, then breathing out, count silently in your mind, 'one'.

After breathing in, then breathing out again, count 'two'.

Continue to count your breaths until 10, then go back to one.

Sometimes you will notice yourself counting higher than 10, which means you got distracted. That's perfectly normal, so just be aware that you got distracted and gently return to counting from one.

Once your mind has settled, you can drop the counting and simply watch the breath.

Noting

Noting your mental process when you get distracted is another technique to help focus the mind on the breath. I learned this technique while I was a monk in Burma.

If you get distracted by thoughts while you are meditating, just say in your mind, slowly, 'Thinking ... thinking ... thinking ...', then go back to the breath.

If you get distracted by outside noise or conversations, say in your mind, slowly, 'Hearing ... hearing ... hearing ...'

If you get bored, acknowledge that you are feeling bored, 'Feeling bored ... feeling bored ... feeling bored ...', then go back to the breath.

The process of noting is helpful because it makes you acknowledge the distraction. Acknowledging the distraction is already training in awareness. Instead of our habitual tendency to dive unconsciously into what distracted us, noting creates a space between us and the distraction.

Thoughts and worries often hijack our attention, especially when we are meditating. Noting that we are 'worrying ... worrying ... worrying ...' allows us to notice the process but not necessarily get swallowed up by the powerful thoughts.

Using phrases

Using phrases can be helpful in calming a busy mind while meditating.

While breathing in, say quietly in your mind, 'Breathing in,' and when breathing out say, 'Breathing out.'

You could even shorten this to saying 'in' when breathing in and 'out' on the outbreath.

Sometimes I use the words 'calm' when breathing in and 'peace' on the outbreath.

A famous verse or gatha by the Vietnamese Zen master, Thích Nhất Hạnh is: 'Breathing in, I calm my body. Breathing out, I smile.'

Duration of practice

For beginners, I suggest at least two to three minutes of mindfulness on the breath to give a taste of the practice. Once the meditator becomes comfortable with a few minutes, they can extend it to 10 minutes. Doing a few minutes daily is much more beneficial than doing 45 minutes once a week or every few weeks. Consistency of practice, even if short, is more important than long but erratic practice.

Be realistic and kind in what it is possible to do daily. Reserving a specific time of the day or night as mindfulness meditation time can help build the practice. In my case, I do it after I wake up, as my mind is calm and alert. Others prefer to do it in the middle of the day or later in the evening. Since all of us have different body clocks, the best time to do a mindfulness practice is when your mind is alert and awake, not when it is dull or fatigued.

The meditation practice should not cause pain or stress. View it as a fun exercise to get to know your mind. Some view it as a relaxation time to get away from the busyness of life. Many experienced daily meditators, including me, spend at least 30 minutes daily doing mindfulness practice. Monks and nuns can spend a few hours every day in sitting meditation practice. At meditation retreats, it is not unusual to spend a total of six to eight hours, spread throughout the day, in sitting meditation practice.

Kind attitude

A kind attitude is a crucial aspect of meditation practice. Kindness to yourself while doing mindfulness practice is so important that Ajahn Brahm, one of my favourite teachers, prefers to call mindfulness *kindfulness*.

I hear many beginner students of mindfulness meditation complain that they cannot meditate because their minds are busy. They try to empty their minds, but their minds just go on and on and on. Expecting your mind to be suddenly still when you meditate is unrealistic.

Emptying your mind is almost impossible when you are a beginner. Noticing that we have busy minds that are out of control, and being at peace with it, being kind to it, will help tame the mind.

Buddhist teachers have taught me that training the mind in mindfulness is similar to training a puppy to sit. Beating the puppy with a stick will just cause harm and resentment. Similarly, with the mind, getting angry and frustrated will not lead to progress. Noticing and accepting that the mind is naturally restless is the first step. Then train it gently with lots of breaks and kindness.

Sleepiness

Sleepiness can be a problem for meditators. It is common for people with busy minds to be sleepy once their mind is calm. However, although sleep is important for physical and mental recovery, it does not lead to psychological progress and maturity.

There are various techniques to manage sleepiness when meditating. The first one is to make sure you have enough sleep at night. If you are sleep-deprived from work, study or staying up too late, you will fall asleep when you are meditating as your body tries to recover from the sleep deficit.

Another technique is to find a time when you are not sleepy. If you are a morning person, it is best to meditate in the morning. If you are an evening person, meditating in the morning can cause sleepiness.

Instead of meditating with your eyes closed, open them halfway and focus on the floor a metre or so away from you – allowing light in can help with alertness.

Some people stand to meditate if sitting meditation makes them feel sleepy. Others do walking meditation instead of sitting.

Walking meditation

When walking, one knows one is walking.
When standing, one knows one is standing.
When sitting, one knows one is sitting.
When lying down, one knows one is lying down.
—the Buddha

· ·

Hack 39: 'Every path, every street in the world is your walking meditation path' —Thích Nhất Hạnh

· ·

Another excellent mindfulness meditation practice is walking meditation. Yes, you can meditate while walking! In the Buddha's words, you can be mindful in all daily activities, including eating, drinking, chewing, savouring, urinating, defecating, walking, standing, sitting, falling asleep, waking up, talking and remaining silent.

I love walking meditation as it trains me to be mindful while in motion. While sitting meditation is excellent for developing clarity and peace, in real life, we do not spend most of our day in a quiet corner paying attention to the breath. Most of us are busy and constantly moving around. Walking meditation helps us develop mindfulness while active.

Many of us walk, or do other activities like showering or washing dishes, without being fully aware of what we are doing. We tend to be in an automatic mode, which is, to be frank, a mindless mode.

Self-reflection

Have you ever driven somewhere and arrived safely at your destination without being able to recall anything about how you got there?

Have you ever turned the shower off and stood there trying to work out whether you've washed your hair or not?

Have you forgotten if you have brushed your teeth or not in the morning?

If any of these things or something similar has ever happened to you, it's probably because the process of driving, showering or toothbrushing has become a reflex, so your mind daydreams while you do it.

Walking meditation is an excellent practice for you to incorporate mindfulness into your daily activities. Having learned walking meditation, it is easy to perform day-to-day activities like cooking, bathing, washing dishes and even playing sport with mindfulness.

Walking meditation is a good alternative to sitting meditation especially when the mind is agitated, restless and anxious. When I notice that my mind is extra busy, I will spend 10 to 15 minutes on walking meditation before I proceed to a sitting meditation.

Practise walking meditation

1. Identify a quiet, private place where you can do your practice.
This is to help you focus and also because it might look weird to anyone who doesn't know what you are doing. At home, I do it in my bedroom or in the backyard.

2. If you can, try walking meditation without footwear. Walking barefoot heightens the perception of walking.

3. Identify a straight path that is at least 10 paces long.
It doesn't need to be any longer as in walking meditation, the focus of our attention is the physical sensation of walking.

The goal is not to get anywhere but to be present in each step.

4. Beginning at one end of the path, stand for a minute in an alert but relaxed position.
Notice the sensation of your feet against the ground.
Notice your breathing.
Your arms can be wherever feels comfortable for you.

5. Raise your right foot to take a step.
Notice the sensation of your right foot lifting, swinging, then landing.

6. As your right foot lands, notice your left foot lifting, swinging and landing.

7. As your left foot lands, notice your right foot lifting and so on.
Your whole attention should be absorbed by the sensation of walking.

8. To avoid stumbling, keep your gaze to the front and not on your feet. Try not to look around as it promotes distraction.
If you get distracted by sights, sounds, thoughts, urges or emotions, just notice and be aware of the distraction, then refocus on the walking.

9. Once you have reached one end of the path, slowly and mindfully turn around, noticing the physical sensation of stopping, standing and turning.

10. Repeat the process of walking, see step 5.

Noting

If my mind is extra busy and restless, I note or label the different actions my feet are engaged in. A simple way to note while doing walking meditation is to think 'right' when the right foot moves, then 'left' when the left foot moves. Noting each stepping motion as 'right' or 'left' anchors your attention to the walking movement. Some people use the word 'step' to note each step taken.

Another noting technique if you want to go deeper into the awareness of walking is to break down the process into several stages. The movement of each foot starts with 'about to lift', then 'lifting', 'swinging', 'landing', 'weight shifting', before the next foot starts its own cycle of 'about to lift', 'lifting', 'swinging', 'landing' and 'weight shifting'.

When you use detailed noting for the first time, start with very slow walking movements. You will not be able to coordinate walking with breathing so drop the focus on your breathing and focus on the sensation of slow walking.

The goal of noting is to be fully immersed in the process of walking. If the noting becomes too distracting, drop it and simply pay attention to the sensation of walking.

Speed

Different Buddhist traditions prefer different speeds of walking meditation. Some walk briskly while others walk in extreme slow motion. My preference is to walk slowly and coordinate my steps with my breathing. Breathing in, I lift my right foot, and breathing out the right foot lands.

Smile

Some meditators can be very serious about their meditation practice to the point that they become stiff, obsessive, scrupulous and perfectionistic. One way to remedy this is to have a half-smile on your face.

Before you start the walking meditation, put on a half-smile. When you are walking, remember to have a half-smile. We can have a fake smile in the beginning but, as our facial muscles are connected to the brain, the half-smile tricks the brain and often relaxes it.

Away from home

The beauty of walking meditation is that, once you have learned it and practised it regularly, you can practise mindfulness while you are walking to your car, in the park or at work. When you practise mindful walking away from the privacy of your home, just walk at a normal pace, with normal movements.

One habit I have developed is to be mindful when I walk from the university car park to my office at the medical school. If no one interrupts me, the walk takes seven minutes. That means I have at least 14 minutes of discreet mindful meditation per day. It also means that by the time I get to my office, I am usually calm, content and clear-headed. Likewise, after a stressful and exhausting day, by the time I get to my car, I am calm, smiling and ready to go home.

Eating meditation

I learned a lot of my mindfulness meditation skills from monks of the Thai Forest Tradition. One of my former teachers was an American monk who established Vimutti Monastery in Auckland. When he said he would teach mindful eating, I got very excited. I love food, especially the Thai, Chinese, Malaysian and Sri Lankan food that is plentiful in the buffets offered by lay supporters of the monastery. Can you imagine developing mindfulness while engaging in your favourite activity?

If I am particularly famished, especially in a monastery where we fast for 16 hours, just the announcement that the meal is ready causes my mind to go into overdrive. Oh, hang on, no! As soon as I wake up, I'm hungry. I check how many hours and minutes it will be before our first meal.

The craving, hungry mind is busy. 'I hope they have the same pad Thai as yesterday. Or I wouldn't mind that chicken curry again. Maybe they'll serve those nice, plump, colourful, sticky Malaysian rice desserts. They were yum!' All these thoughts, cravings and wishes swirl through my mind before I even see the buffet table.

In mindful eating, as in other mindfulness practices, we become aware of the various musicians – sight, sound, taste, hearing, touch and mind – in our stage of awareness. All of these senses will be engaged in eating meditation, but the taste and mind musicians tend to be the stars of the show.

The practice of mindful eating has been very revealing to me. There are so many things going on in my mind when confronted by something I love and have huge cravings for. The practice also shines light on the opposite of craving, which is hating or pushing away.

I notice that I tend to have expectations that, when not fulfilled, result in disappointment. I also notice that when I am open to experience with minimal expectation, the experience becomes delightful, fun and satisfying. You can learn this and much more just from eating meditation.

Self-reflection

Before you are about to have a meal or better yet, select food from a buffet, even before you see the food, what is going on with your mind?

What thoughts are you having?

What are you craving?

What are your wishes and desires?

Remember, this is a mindfulness practice, a practice of awareness. Be aware of thoughts, cravings, feelings, sensations. No judgments, please. Allow the mind to perform its crazy processes and just be aware.

Practise mindful eating

Chew mindfully.

Notice the urge to stuff things in your mouth without giving in to it.

Be open to different smells, colours, shapes, tastes and textures.

Be thankful for the nourishment, regardless of whether the food is delicious or not.

Be grateful for all the people responsible for growing, harvesting, selling, delivering, buying and cooking all of the items in your food.

> Be grateful for the countless lives that were taken in order to nourish us – mammals, birds, fish and even the insects that died in the growing and harvesting of grains, vegetables and fruits.

In a Thai Forest monastery, mealtimes are special because monks and nuns fast for at least 16 hours. They are the first in the queue for meals. After the monastics, it's the turn of the lay people.

As I stand in the queue, I notice what my mind does. 'Do I want to be at the front of the queue because I am hungry? Should I suppress the desire to be at the front because I don't want people to think that I am a glutton and not practising restraint?'

Notice the interplay of various thoughts and motivations in the mind.

Sometimes I get annoyed at ending up in the middle or at the end of the queue as it means I might miss out on dessert. Thoughts of self-righteousness have me thinking that I should be closer to the front and daytime visitors should be at the back.

I notice my angry thoughts, smile and let them go.

When I reach the buffet table, my excitement level goes up a notch. I notice a slight increase in my heart rate. My mouth salivates as I take in the array of dishes in front of me.

This is a mindful practice. I notice my body touching the edge of the buffet table, my hand holding the serving spoon, the movement of my arm reaching for the rice, my thoughts going berserk with the sight of all these gorgeous foods.

I am now in front of the dessert table. I am feeling heady with the choice of delicious, colourful desserts in front of me. I notice that I do not have much space left on my plate. Disappointment sets in.

This is a mindfulness exercise. The mind is aware and alert – noticing my moment-by-moment experience. I notice the craving, the judgments, the conversations, the kind thoughts, the sense of self-righteousness – all before even eating the food.

As I sit at the table, I mindfully note the various sensory experiences that are at play. I see the food on my plate. I smell the aromas of spices. I watch my mind crave, wondering what I should eat first.

As I eat, I count the number of times I chew my food. In mindful eating, this is a technique used to anchor the mind to the present. I average 20 to 30 chewing motions per bite when mindful – but fewer when I am not.

After only three chews, I notice my fork going in for more. I notice my craving mind wanting to get another hit of this beautiful pad Thai. I decide to continue chewing until I reach 30.

In mindfulness, one notices what the mind does. Desire arises and we quench it. Then desire comes back in a different form. We get excited by new things, but once we obtain them, we move on and crave other things. We shove new experiences in, wanting another hit, and another, and another.

From mindfulness, we develop insight that desire is relentless and filling it up never finishes. Perhaps giving in to desires all the time is not the answer. A mindful way is to notice desire arise and watch it pass away.

· . · . · . · . · . · . · . · . · . · . · . · . · . · . · . · . · . · . · .

Hack 40: The next time you're eating, try being mindful to see how crazy and busy the mind is.

· . · . · . · . · . · . · . · . · . · . · . · . · . · . · . · . · . · . · .

With mindful eating, we develop insights into how powerful craving is and how it can rule our lives. We learn how to develop restraint by not acting impulsively while getting food or while eating. We can witness joy, exhilaration, excitement and unfulfilled expectations. There can even be thoughts of violence and feelings of compassion. All from eating meditation.

Later, with regular practice, it will become less chaotic than this. The mind becomes more restrained, calmer and at peace.

Dishwashing meditation

Thích Nhất Hạnh, one of the most influential Zen masters of my lifetime, was famous for applying mindfulness in our daily activities. His teachings influenced my mindfulness practice immensely as he made mindfulness practice fun, light and effortless.

I particularly like his dishwashing meditation instructions as they are simple and yet profound:

To my mind, the idea that doing dishes is unpleasant can occur only when you aren't doing them. Once you are standing in front of the sink with your sleeves rolled up and your hands in the warm water, it is really quite pleasant.

I enjoy taking my time with each dish, being fully aware of the dish, the water and each movement of my hands. I know that if I hurry in order to be able to finish so I can sit down sooner and eat dessert or enjoy a cup of tea, the time of washing dishes will be unpleasant and not worth living. That would be a pity, for each minute, each second of life is a miracle. The dishes themselves and the fact that I am here washing them are miracles!

If I am incapable of washing dishes joyfully, if I want to finish them quickly so I can go and have dessert or a cup of tea, I will be equally incapable of enjoying my dessert or my tea when I finally have them.

I must confess it takes me a bit longer to do the dishes, but I live fully in every moment, and I am happy.

Washing the dishes is at the same time a means and an end. We do the dishes not only in order to have clean dishes, but we also do the dishes just to do the dishes, to live fully in each moment while washing them, and to be truly in touch with life.

Mindfulness in day-to-day activities

You will have gathered by now that an attitude of mindfulness can be incorporated into other activities outside 'formal' meditation sessions like sitting, walking and eating meditations. When I learned of Thích Nhất Hạnh's approach to mindfulness, which is to apply it to all our daily activities, mindfulness became fun, practical and less of a chore.

With an attitude of being aware and peacefully accepting of the sensations of the body, feelings and thoughts, day-to-day activities can be performed mindfully. Apart from dishwashing meditation, my other favourites include showering, cooking and swimming meditation.

While showering, I notice the movement of my hand slowly turning on the tap. I feel the coldness of the metal against my fingers. There is an initial shock from the water soaking my body. I feel grateful for the gift of water that comes out of the tap. I tip a few drops of shampoo on my hand. I slowly lather my scalp. I soap my body and notice the bubbles on my skin. I wash the shampoo and soap off, noticing the sensation of water cleansing my skin. Instead of quickly hopping out of the shower and drying myself, towelling myself dry can be a whole mindful experience.

Cooking meditation begins with consciously preparing the ingredients, from taking them out of the pantry and the fridge, to measuring, cutting and slicing mindfully. While stir-frying, I notice the heat of the wok, smell the aromatics, hold the wooden spatula, stir, mix and taste.

Being grateful for the gift of gas (or electricity), the gift of having all the ingredients and cooking utensils available and the ability to cook can make mindful cooking more meaningful.

I like to swim in the open water, and when I am not mindful, I notice that I daydream even when in the middle of the sea! Fortunately, I have not drowned yet because of my mindlessness. When I remember to mindfully swim, I use noting, counting or feeling. While doing a right stroke, I note it as 'right', and same with the left. Sometimes, I count my strokes up to six, followed by sighting or looking out of the water. Feeling involves noticing the sensation of the water against my head, face, neck, arms, body and legs.

Mindfulness has been successfully incorporated into other sports, including running, golf, bowling, tennis, football and even rugby. The principles are the same. The player pays attention to the sensations in their body, their thoughts and their emotions while engaged in sports. As a result, papañca or overthinking is put in check.

Mindfulness meditation has been credited by top athletes in basketball, football, rugby, tennis and golf as crucial to their winning performances. Mindfulness allows athletes to be present in the moment, mainly in their breath and their body, while avoiding the unhelpful rumination and overthinking that can ruin their game. Being mindful has resulted in having the extra mental edge and clarity that are essential for optimal sports performance. With mindfulness practice, winning and losing are experienced calmly as temporary states. When mindful, all our experiences, like the breath, just come and go.

Mindfulness of feelings and emotions

The Buddha gave specific instructions on how to be mindful to feelings and emotions. He said, 'And how, monks, does a monk dwell contemplating feelings in feelings? Here, when feeling a pleasant feeling, a monk understands: "I feel a pleasant feeling"; when feeling a painful feeling, he understands: "I feel a painful feeling"; when feeling a neutral feeling, he understands: "I feel a neutral feeling" … he dwells contemplating in feelings their nature of both arising and vanishing.'

In Buddhism, feelings and emotions are not the same thing. Feeling is pleasurable, neutral or unpleasant. Our reactions to these feelings constitute emotions.

We feel anxious, angry, annoyed, upset and exasperated to the point of wanting to throttle someone out of frustration. We also feel joy, contentment, gratitude, connection, compassion, exhilaration, excitement and inspiration. Being human involves various feeling and emotional states.

Hack 41: If we do not engage with them, emotions and feelings just arise and pass away.

Feelings and emotions typically last a short time, with one scientist, Jill Bolte Taylor, suggesting that after a negative emotion is triggered, it takes 90 seconds for the brain to rinse it out. In other words, negative emotions trigger a surge of brain neurochemicals that then dissipate in 90 seconds. This finding is consistent with classic Buddhist teachings that emotions are impermanent and always changing.

Some view emotions, particularly negative emotions, as bad. Emotions are neither good nor bad; they are just features of being a highly evolved mammal. Complications and suffering arise not from emotions but from how we respond or relate to them.

When we experience negative emotions, we unconsciously feed and fertilise them. Having been annoyed by a flippant comment made by our significant other, our mind revisits the comment repeatedly, then drags up other negative comments they've made in the past, adding other stories about when our partner hasn't been so nice to us.

From one comment that we could have easily ignored for 90 seconds, we now feel angry and upset.

Andy

Some of us see negative emotions as bad and try to avoid experiencing them. Andy was an accomplished property developer who, for no obvious reason, decided to end his life by crashing his car into oncoming traffic. Fortunately, the truck on the other side of the road swerved and Andy drove into a thick bush, saving his life.

In therapy, it became apparent that Andy had suppressed most of his negative emotions. His wife had been cheating on him and his two young children were not doing well in school. At home, Andy forced himself to be cheerful and optimistic. He deluded himself that everything would be sorted out eventually.

As a child, his father had chided him for crying and for showing sadness or anger as they were deemed to be unmanly responses. Until the crash, Andy had perfected his technique for emotional suppression. He kept himself positive all the time even if, internally, he was suffering hugely.

Therapy with Andy focused on normalising emotions, and acknowledging and befriending both positive and negative emotions.

It's perfectly normal to feel anger, sadness and fear. They are often fleeting. They signal to us that something is not going right.

Bullying emotions

I have had numerous patients who have had difficulties managing their emotions. I also know several people who I'd rather avoid when they're on an emotional rampage.

A doctor colleague of mine, who had suffered from emotional dysregulation since she was a teenager, said to me, 'Tony, I need help. My emotions bully me.'

Poor emotional regulation causes tremendous suffering not just to the person who experiences it but also the people who love them.

For many of my patients who have dysregulated emotions, mindfulness has been a saviour. It has allowed them to notice emotions and let them be.

In due course, as confirmed by Jill Bolte Taylor, emotions will dissipate. They have a purpose, so pushing them down does not help. Focusing on them and feeding them, on the other hand, prolongs them.

Practise emotional mindfulness

When you are feeling emotions, for example, sadness, be aware and name what you are feeling.

'This is the feeling of sadness.'

Be curious about it.

What triggered it?

'The horrible comment made by my son triggered the sadness.'

What does your body feel now?

'I can feel a heaviness in my abdomen, my throat is parched, I can sense my eyes welling up.'

Acknowledge it and be kind to it.

'This is feeling sadness and it's okay, it's normal to be sad given the situation.'

Recognise the impermanence of emotions.

'Sadness arose, Sadness will pass away.'

Recognise that you are not your emotions.

'I am not my sadness and sadness is not me. It's just part of a flow of experiences that arise and pass away.'

Another technique, which is now being taught in schools, is Jill Bolte Taylor's 90-second approach.

When confronted by strong negative emotions, grab hold of your watch or phone and use it to count to 90.

During that time, try not revisit the emotion or create stories.

Combine the 90-second count with mindful breathing as this will naturally calm your body.

CHAPTER 11

Building your mindfulness muscle

Developing a regular mindfulness practice is hard. It took me several attempts and many years before I became committed to meditating daily. It is not that different from learning a new musical instrument or deciding to go to the gym regularly. In the beginning, we have lots of zeal, then our enthusiasm wanes. Here are a few tips to help you build a regular mindfulness practice.

1. Join a meditation group that meets regularly

Many people use apps, video clips or books to gain basic understanding of how to meditate. This is very different from the way meditators have learned mindfulness practice for most of the past 2600 years. Before the advent of the internet and smartphone technology, meditators learned from teachers and practised in communities together.

Meditating with other people, who are committed to it, gives one a boost in motivation to practise further. This provides a degree of accountability as other people will check in with you if you don't turn up.

It might be the result of a placebo effect or some kind of real psychic energy, but my meditations seem deeper when I am practising in a group.

Try to find a local group, which can be Buddhist or non-Buddhist, it does not really matter. What matters is that you belong to a community of mindfulness meditators, people who value their quality and clarity of mind.

I know some meditators who are active in their online meditation groups. While a face-to-face physical group is preferred, an online group is an alternative.

2. Find an experienced meditation teacher

Throughout your meditation adventure, you will have countless questions regarding technique. Common questions include what to do with boredom, sleepiness and a super-distracted mind. Dr Google or ChatGPT might give you answers to your questions, but an experienced meditation teacher will give you an answer based on both their knowledge *and* experience.

When I do sitting meditation, I usually sit on a thick cushion and begin with a straight but relaxed back. After 10 or 20 minutes of paying attention to the breath and the body, I notice my back slump very gradually and it ends up curved and slouched.

I searched the internet and various meditation books to find a solution for this. One source suggested I straighten my back as soon as I noticed it slouching. Another suggested that I just observe and let it be.

When I visited Amaravati Monastery outside of London in 2017, I asked the abbot there, Ajahn Amaro, about my back conundrum. His answer was simple, practical, yet profound: 'See what happens if you let your back slouch. Observe your mind. Then straighten your back and see what happens to your mind.'

His answer was empirical and based on wisdom. He did not tell me exactly what to do with my back. He wanted me to experiment and develop insights based on my own observations. I wouldn't have got that kind of answer from Dr Google or a paid app.

You might be curious as to what I do now. When I notice my back slouching, I notice the sensation of my slouched back, then gradually straighten it in a relaxed and mindful fashion. This is because I observed that when I let my back slouch, my mind tends to get dull and lazy. Straightening it, with kindness and without judgment, enhances my attention and increases my alertness.

3. Commit to daily practice

For meditation practice to become a habit, regularity and consistency is key. Setting a regular time to meditate will yield better results that just meditating when you find time.

Meditating based on your level of enthusiasm and motivation is a guaranteed killer of your practice. In the same way, going to my swim training with the squad based on how I feel when my alarm goes off early in the morning would result in zero attendance.

Motivation and feelings are overrated as a cause for behavioural change. Commitment will yield better results. Commit to meditating, even for a few minutes, at the same time of day and ideally in the same place or spot.

By doing this, you are developing a habit. Even just a few minutes, every day, will build you a more durable mindfulness muscle than big bursts of 60-minute meditations once a week or every few weeks.

4. Manage your expectations

In the early days of my mindfulness adventure, I found teachers who said, 'Do not have expectations when meditating,' which I found annoying and unrealistic. If I did not have expectations, I wouldn't be meditating at all!

Only later did that statement make sense to me. Of course, I hoped that meditation would make me calmer, gentler and more compassionate. However, in the actual practice of meditation, while you are doing it, not having expectations is crucial.

Mindfulness is about being open to whatever you are experiencing. You might be distracted sometimes and concentrated and peaceful at other times. Both are helpful meditations. But if you expect to be peaceful or to have sublime psychic experiences, then you are not practising mindfulness properly. I can guarantee that you will have a tough meditation because your mind is craving for something in the future and is not living in the present.

Joseph Goldstein, a well-regarded mindfulness teacher in the US, shared a particular mantra that I still use, especially if I have a busy mind: 'Everything arises and passes away, there is nothing to want.' Repeating those words slowly at the beginning of a meditation practice settles my mind and whittles away the expectation that my mind should be at peace. In not having expectations, my expectations of peace are often met. It takes a bit of mental gymnastics, but you will get it when you observe your mind mindfully.

5. Use apps and websites

There is a clear role for apps and meditation websites in mindfulness practice. I use the app Insight Timer to time my daily meditations. It also records my meditation duration and frequency, which can be helpful in motivating me to meditate. It also has an online community and recordings of various meditation teachers. However, because it is not specifically a mindfulness app, it has a lot of other types of meditations from many traditions, which can confuse a beginner. Sometimes having too many choices can result in learning a few techniques superficially but not deeply.

I also recommend several mindfulness apps, including Headspace, Waking Up and 10% Happier. Headspace is an amazing app and is one of the most downloaded meditation apps in the world. Like Insight Timer, it has branched out into other techniques and approaches, which can cause confusion.

I created the website www.calm.auckland.ac.nz back in 2007. It has a repository of classic guided mindfulness and loving kindness meditations recorded by esteemed teachers like Vidyamala Burch and Sharon Salzberg. Despite its age, thousands of users still access it regularly.

My concern about using apps is that many of them are designed to hook you and make you dependent on them. I am sure the main motivation of many developers and owners of meditation apps is altruistic, but once money becomes involved, many of these apps will want you to rely on them. My suggestion is to use them occasionally and try meditating on your own without them. I have met people who are unable to meditate without using their mobile apps. You do not want to become one of them.

On the flipside, I have benefited hugely from podcast programmes like *Insight Hour* by Joseph Goldstein, the Amaravati Buddhist Monastery's podcast and the Buddhist Society of Western Australia's podcast. Online, I can access talks, lectures, meditation workshops by various top-notch meditation teachers. These can be accessed using any podcast application.

Smartphones = mindlessness

The ability to pay attention is one of our greatest resources as highly evolved primates. With attention, we can notice our experience, analyse, plan, review, reflect and handle stressors. As well as being one of the main Buddhist practices that will make us happier and lessen our suffering, mindfulness aims to enhance our attention and our ability to attend to the present moment.

Smartphones are increasingly becoming seen as the enemy of attention training or mindfulness. One Buddhist monk jokingly said, 'The smartphone is the devil in your pocket.'

I thought that sounded extreme and narrow-minded until I started to see in myself how the smartphone controls my attention. From the moment I'd wake up, I'd pick up my phone to check the time. Then I'd look to see if there were any important messages in my various messaging apps. Then I'd check my emails. Mindlessly, I'd start scrolling through my favourite news outlets checking local New Zealand news, CNN, BBC, *The Guardian* and Al Jazeera.

After about 15 minutes, I'd move to Facebook and mindlessly scroll through posts and unending reels, most of which were meaningless and a waste of time. Thirty minutes later, I'd find myself rushing to get in the shower, so I could meditate before I headed to work.

Throughout the day, in between patients, I'd go through the same rigmarole of clicking on my messaging apps, news outlets and social media. If there was still time, I'd go back to the messaging apps in case I'd missed a crucial message in the past five minutes.

These days, I am better at managing my phone. I still check my messages as soon as I get up but I avoid the various news outlets and social media. At work, during downtimes, I notice the urge to check my phone and try to be mindful by just noticing the urge.

There's slight discomfort that I might be missing out on something if I do not check my phone. I watch the urge and eventually the urge goes away. Sometimes, I still grab my phone but instead of clicking on my favourite apps, I click on *Access to Insight*, an app that houses the Buddhist scriptures.

I still have a very tight relationship with my phone. When the battery reaches a critically low level, I experience mild panic. But I know that the world will continue, somewhat, even if my phone is dead for the next couple of hours.

Smartphones have transformed the lives of billions of people. At our fingertips, we can be a witness to what is going on around the world, transfer money across continents, communicate with loved ones for free, check the latest stock market reports, play video games, watch movies and television shows, listen to whatever music we want and even meditate with the Dalai Lama.

There is no question that smartphones have transformed our lives and made them richer and easier. However, there is accumulating evidence of the destructive effects of smartphones. As a sleep specialist, I instruct many of my insomnia patients to put down their phones at least two hours before they go to bed. The damage blue light from mobile phones does to sleep is proven. Smartphone use has also been linked to increasing rates of depression and anxiety among young people.

Evidence of the effects of smartphones on mind*less*ness, the opposite of mindfulness, is slowly accumulating. Most of this evidence is anecdotal but a recent study of 668 university students in the US showed that smartphone use is strongly associated with mindlessness.

Mindlessness is associated with easy distractibility, impatience, low mood, anxiety, poor emotional regulation and being lost in thought.

For many young people, teenagers in particular, the smartphone has become an extra body part, something that they are literally and figuratively connected with for most of the day. This extra appendage allows users to access information and perform functions in an instant. If the smartphone is perceived to be slow, tempers flare and patience goes out the window. Imagine sending a message to someone you are going out with and knowing that the person has seen your message but has not responded in the past 10 minutes. Chaos!

The smartphone has been specifically designed to grab and hold the user's attention such that when the surroundings are not interesting enough, the user automatically grabs the phone to look for something more interesting. In restaurants, classrooms, buses and trains, people are glued to their phones. Real conversations and interactions with other humans are now boring, so friends, parents, siblings and lovers have been replaced by the devil in our pockets.

A visiting monk in our local monastery told meditators that the smartphone is a machine that will destroy our mindfulness. The more we use it, the less we can pay attention to the present, the less we can be mindful throughout the day. He does not need to remind me. I have seen it happen to me.

· ·

Hack 42: Cut back your use of mobile phones if you want to enhance your mindfulness.

· ·

At many mindfulness meditation retreats, mobile phones are now banned. They can only be accessed at the end of the retreat. If there are home emergencies, family members can contact the retreat organiser. Still, a few meditation retreat participants hide their contraband phones in their cars and check them in the evenings.

Yuval Harari, the author of the bestselling book *Sapiens*, is one of the most respected philosophers, historians and thinkers in the world. He admits that he does not own a smartphone. He values his time and attention. He says mobile phones have too much drawing power and destructive effects on attention.

If attention training is our goal, we must revisit our relationship with our smartphones.

Is the end goal of Buddhist practice to be mindful?

The short answer is no. The goal of Buddhist practice is the cessation of suffering. Mindfulness is just one of the eight paths identified by the Buddha in the Noble Eightfold Path. The Eightfold Path is a mental and ethical guideline developed by the Buddha for the relief of suffering and attainment of happiness. In addition to mindfulness, the other seven paths include right understanding, intention, speech, action, livelihood, effort and concentration. Engaging in mindfulness here and there might offer some stress relief but not total cessation of suffering.

In my experience, mindfulness has made me a bit calmer, less reactive and less impulsive. Emotions do not overrun me as much as they once did. I am a little bit more present. I am more aware of the rising and passing of experiences, thoughts, emotions and sensations. I am grateful for all of these positive effects from years of mindfulness practice.

However, there is one effect of mindfulness that definitely lessens my suffering. When I am annoyed, irritated or upset, I notice mindfully my experience. Then, I ask myself, 'Tony, what are you clinging to? What are you pushing away?'

In that moment, I become conscious of the unpleasant feeling, and I have the option to cross the bridge to clinging or pushing away, which then results in suffering.

Let me explain further.

In the Buddha's teachings, he identified craving, clinging or pushing away as the main cause of suffering. It is when we are not accepting of the present moment, when we want things to be different, when we push away what is going on or crave for more of what we are experiencing; that is when suffering and dissatisfaction arise.

For example, if I drive mindlessly and someone cuts me off, I get upset. While upset, my mind goes into overdrive, hating these idiotic drivers, creating fantasies that annual driving tests should be mandatory, that all our cars should be monitored by Big Brother so that unskilled driving can be punished. I then start blaming the road works department because our highways in New Zealand are relatively primitive compared to those in Australia and the US. From an initial upset, I am now raging, so I chase the driver who cut me off.

If I am mindful, I notice that someone has just cut me off. I feel upset but I notice the feeling of upset. The feeling of upset comes and goes so I just let 'upset' do its thing. I am accepting of the present moment and do not cross into the next phase, which is wanting things to be different *now*. It is in the wanting things to be different *now* that causes dissatisfaction and suffering.

Of course, wanting things to be different in the future makes sense, but it is in the craving and demanding that the experience should be different *now* that causes suffering. Being mindful allows the mind to notice the present upsetting situation and accept it peacefully, as nothing can be done to change the situation in this moment. There is less suffering or no suffering at all. There is peace.

CHAPTER 12

Living simply

Followers of the Buddha try to cultivate certain virtues or personal qualities that aid in the liberation from anxiety, stress and suffering. These include generosity, truthfulness and mindfulness.

However, one quality that many non–Buddhists shy away from is the virtue of renunciation. Even just hearing (or reading) the word renunciation turns many people off because it conjures up images of ascetics who live in caves, sleep on the ground and have meagre possessions. Renunciation is seen as anathema to what western commercialism espouses, which is a life of ultimate comfort, pampering and luxury.

Renunciation does not mean giving up possessions or living as a pauper. It has nothing to do with being wealthy or poor. A person can be very poor and still be attached to the few things he has left, for example a spoon, fork, knife and plate, to the point that he clutches them when he sleeps. That person is not living a renunciant's life. On the other hand, a person can be surrounded by comfort and luxury, but if their mind is detached and not enslaved by their possessions, then they might be living a life of renunciation.

The word renunciation has so much baggage and misunderstanding attached to it that I've chosen instead to use the terms 'living simply' or 'holding things lightly'. It refers to the ability to let go of our attachments when the time comes.

The goal of renunciation is to change our relationships with objects, people, concepts, ideas and beliefs. From owning them, attaching to them and falsely believing that they define us, we learn how to relate to them simply as phenomena that come and go. Holding them lightly, we are open to letting go. With letting go comes freedom, peace, happiness and contentment.

Simple monk life

In January 2017, I committed myself to being a temporary Buddhist monk at Chanmyay Myaing Meditation Centre outside of Yangon, in Burma. I had been meditating on and off since 2004 and had always wondered what it would be like to dive into the Buddha's teachings head on, no holds barred, doing the full thing. I had attended retreats at which I'd meditated for many days, and lived kindly and simply. But something nagged at me to do the full 'monk thing'.

What attracted me, as well as scared me, was the extreme simplicity of the life of a monk. They follow a simple daily schedule of chores, meals, meditation and chanting.

As a monk, I couldn't leave the monastery unless it was important, and I had to ask permission to do so. I had to give up my phone, though urgent phone calls and texts were allowed. There was no Wi-Fi or none that I was aware of. I had a basic room, painted green with one window. I was fortunate to have my own toilet and shower area. My wooden bed had a very thin mattress with an accompanying malnourished pillow. There was no other furniture, pictures or decorations. There were no mirrors or even images of the Buddha.

I was given two sets of robes, a towel and an alms bowl. My hair was shaved, and we were not allowed to have watches or any adornments. After being ordained as a monk, the locals gave me toothpaste, a toothbrush, some soap, a face towel and some tablets for headaches and stomach aches.

Each morning, we were woken up by a giant gong at around 5am. This was followed by a quiet breakfast, then we prepared for our alms rounds in the village. In single file, the monks walked around the village barefoot, collecting our lunch from the villagers. Back at the monastery, we ate our lunch, which was followed by chores and meditation for the rest of the day. I was back in my room ready for bed around 10pm.

For many monasteries throughout Burma, Thailand, Laos and Sri Lanka, this is the routine followed by hundreds of thousands of monks and nuns every day until they die.

Those two weeks living a life of a renunciant, someone who has renounced or given up the material world, were some of the best I'd ever had.

There are many possible reasons for this, with living simply at the top of the list. Being able to detoxify myself from my various 'addictions' was a refreshing experience.

The Buddha asked his monks to follow a code that covered all aspects of conduct, behaviour and practicalities. The code was called the Vinaya. It had 227 rules for the monk in the Theravadan tradition.

In the Vinaya, the Buddha was very specific regarding food, clothing, possessions and shelter for his monks and nuns. In his wisdom, the rules were formulated not to deliberately make a monk's life hard. Instead, the rules were designed to simplify life, allowing monks and nuns to change their often-complicated relationship with the material world, to live simply so that they had more time to focus on training the mind.

Food, glorious food

For monks, food was to be consumed mindfully and in moderate amounts. We meditated while eating. There was no chit-chat. Eating was done only to sustain the body, not to indulge the sense organs.

As a monk, I didn't have much choice anyway as all of our food was donated. We didn't have a menu from which to choose our meals. I was lucky in that the monasteries I stayed at had generous donors, so we never wanted for good food. In poorer monasteries, of which there are many, monks survive on sticky rice and vegetables, with the occasional protein, all donated by locals.

There was emphasis on gratitude for the food, those who donated it, prepared it and all the countless causes and conditions (rain, soil, sun, air, seeds, birds, bees, farmers, distributors, previous generations of farmers, villagers, cooks, soy sauce makers, logistics and so on) that allowed the food to be offered to us.

Monks and nuns of the Theravadan tradition also practise an ancient form of intermittent fasting. There is a six-hour window for eating between breakfast and lunch. No food can be consumed after midday. If we were hungry, we were encouraged to notice the hunger and not to fear it. This was a huge challenge for me as I'd always got migraines when I missed meals.

After my first three days of the Buddha's intermittent fasting protocol, my body got used to feeling hungry and my brain did not panic and develop headaches. We were allowed to drink as much water as we wanted, and we were also allowed tea and coffee.

In some monasteries, including the one I stayed in outside Yangon, at 5pm we were offered a very thick and super-sweet fruit juice that adequately soothed hunger pangs.

One afternoon, I got extremely annoyed when a monk called for a meeting just before juice time, which meant possibly forgoing the juice. Obviously, I still needed to do a lot of work on letting go, but I was mindful of it.

After the meeting, I rushed to the cafeteria in hope that the juice would be waiting for me. As expected, there was no juice. The kitchen staff followed a strict schedule, and the tables were cleaned by 5.30pm.

After four stints as a temporary monk in strict Buddhist monasteries where the rules of the Vinaya are followed, my relationship with food has changed. I still love food and plan my social life around it. However, lack of food or hunger does not scare me anymore. I can delay or forgo a meal without making a big song and dance about it. I do not get hunger-related migraines anymore.

Last year, my doctor told me that I needed to do something to bring my blood sugar down. He suggested that I start on metformin, a common first medication for diabetes, even though I was only in the early stages of pre-diabetes.

I told him to give me three months to bring my blood sugar down using exercise and healthier eating. I instituted a strict eight-hour window during which I could eat, something that would have been very difficult if I hadn't had my monastery training. After three months, my blood sugar normalised and I lost six kilograms. I still follow a modified version of this eating schedule now, even though my health has improved.

Fasting or restricting food intake is not only practised by Buddhists. Many religions include fasting or abstaining from certain foods as part of their practice. Catholics fast and abstain from eating meat on certain days during Lent as a way of sharing in Christ's suffering. In Islam, fasting involves no food or water from dawn to sunset for the month of Ramadan.

Despite the different reasons for fasting, in both religions, fasting is also seen as enhancing self-discipline, self-restraint and cultivating gratitude and patience – the same reasons Buddhist monks and nuns fast daily.

We are all addicts

Humans like to feel good and experience pleasure and comfort as often as possible, which is sometimes at odds with living simply. When we discover that certain activities or objects make us feel good, we try to engage in them more and more. We get hooked on shopping, collecting, eating, watching TV or movies, sex, playing sports or video games. We get addicted to substances, pornography and gambling. Many of us get addicted to people and relationships because of how they make us feel. In a more subtle way, without us being aware, we get addicted to ideas, concepts, ideologies and religious teachings. We get so attached to them that we start to see anyone else with a different view as wrong and, in extreme cases, think that they should be put aside, punished, or even killed!

With mindfulness practice, I am more aware of my own addictions. Fortunately, I do not have serious ones, but I have many moderate addictions.

I have a moderate addiction to Asian food. Given the choice, I will eat it more than 90 per cent of the time unless I am in Europe. If told that I cannot have Asian food, I will experience some disappointment, but I will manage (most of the time).

Recently, I was at a weekend market where there were many stalls selling beautiful French, Italian, Spanish and New Zealand food, but I ended up going to a Malaysian place selling stir-fried noodles.

I also have a moderate addiction to Bach's music and European period dramas on TV. I used to have a moderate addiction to collecting Buddha statues, but I have successfully managed that by giving some of my favourite pieces to friends and family.

There was even a brief period when, as a senior doctor, I got hooked on a video game called *Age of Empires* to the point that I was playing it until two or three in the morning. It took me some effort to stop playing it. Since then, I have not installed strategy games that involve building civilisations and commanding armies on my laptop as I know that I have a weakness or addictive predisposition for them.

When I was younger, I had a strong and unhealthy addiction to my Catholic faith. I was obsessed with the church's teachings and viewed anyone who was a non-believer as wrong. I believed that they would suffer eternal damnation. At that time, I was not even open to discussing other views, as I perceived that to be a waste of energy. My mind was closed and blinded by my views.

In the past few years, I've noticed my addiction to my smartphone. My phone-checking behaviour gets more intense if there are serious events going on in the world.

I sometimes notice that after checking my email, messages and favourite news outlets, I go back to emails and messages in just a few minutes. I have become addicted to the process of checking!

Addiction to relationships

It is easy to understand how we as humans can get addicted to objects, feelings, recreational substances, food or activities. What many of us do not realise is that we also get addicted to people, because other people can make us feel good, complete or important. It is perfectly normal to care for and love people who are close to us. However, there is a point after which what we thought was love becomes an unhealthy attachment, a possession and an addiction.

Alicia and Anthony

Alicia and Anthony met at a meditation retreat in Sydney. They were both in their late twenties, single and working as nurses at a Sydney hospital. Both were tired of the dating app scene so meeting each other at the retreat was an unexpected bonus. Both felt they had found their true 'soulmate'.

They got married less than a year after meeting, and everyone thought theirs was a match made in heaven. They were inseparable and seemed intoxicated by each other.

However, a few months after the wedding, Alicia's friends and family became worried. She was not the ebullient life of the party she had once been. In fact, she hadn't been attending their regular family get-togethers. On the rare occasion she showed up, she stayed less than an hour and had to rush back home.

With Alicia's mother's birthday coming up, her sisters noticed that she was withdrawn. Usually, Alicia would be the instigator of the birthday programme, but she showed little interest in being involved. On the day of the party, they thought it was curious that their sister was wearing a long-sleeved shirt in the middle of summer. When Alicia was rushing to leave the party, her sisters confronted her and demanded to know what was going on.

Alicia showed them the bruises on her arms. Her relationship with Anthony had turned into a living nightmare. He was physically abusive if Alicia came home a minute late. He had become very controlling of her movements outside their home. He checked her emails and phone messages to see if she had talked to other men. He had threatened to kill Alicia if he found any evidence of infidelity.

Their relationship hadn't started out this way. In the beginning, she had been very happy with Anthony, as he was tender, caring and treated her like a princess. There were a few instances when Anthony told her that she was so precious to him that he couldn't imagine life without her. Hearing this in the beginning made Alicia feel good, but, later, this meant she had become a possession to him.

To keep Anthony happy, she would constantly reassure him of her love and unquestionable fidelity. She interpreted Anthony's violent tendencies and possessiveness as a form of intense love. She protected Anthony from her family because she knew that they would not understand the powerful bond that they shared.

After some significant pressure from her family, the couple engaged a relationship counsellor, and after a year, they parted ways.

People sometimes get addicted or attached to other people because of how the other person makes them feel. Being with the other person quenches a deep thirst for completeness. This doesn't just happen in intimate relationships. Some parents believe that they own their children, and that children are there to fulfil a role in their lives. This is no different from the relationship between Anthony and Alicia. Some parents control their children, monitor their every move, micromanage their school and social activities and isolate them from other children. In extreme cases, children have been beaten by their parents because they have flouted the rules.

These are forms of attachments that have gone overboard, often masked as love, care or devotion.

Many of us are romantics and believe, rightly or wrongly, that our relationship with our partner will be forever. That is a tough expectation and is inconsistent with nature. If you strip away the romance and delusional beliefs in relationships, and factor in impermanence – that everything is in flux and constantly changing – what you are left with is the truth that anything can happen in a relationship.

Couples change, from how they look, to their health, to their love for each other. There will be huge challenges to relationships, emanating from the couples themselves or from the outside.

Life is finite. If the relationship lasts for a long time, one partner will eventually die before the other. There can be no 'forever' in our world.

If we accept that all aspects of our relationships are in flux, we become less addicted to each other. Our expectations become more realistic. We loosen our addiction to the ideal.

However, despite the impermanence, if there is deep understanding and compassion for each other, regardless of all the changes that go on, then the chances of the relationship thriving and lasting for a long time are higher. But to expect that everything will remain the same from the moment you laid eyes on each other is unrealistic, delusional and setting yourself up for failure.

When both individuals come to the realisation that, despite their sincere efforts, the relationship is not viable and is causing them harm, they need to acknowledge impermanence. They should embrace the ability to move forward with kindness and understanding, starting a new chapter in their lives free from toxic resentment.

Take your relationships seriously, invest in them deeply, but hold your expectations lightly. If necessary, despite your best efforts, you may have to let go. Remembering the Buddha's teachings on kindness, at the very least, minimise harm to yourself and your partner.

Addiction to ideas, views, beliefs and achievements

One addiction I need to continually work on is my addiction to thinking I am right. I am judgmental towards others who are doing things 'wrong' or who do not know any better. I get annoyed when people do not follow the processes I expect.

Many years ago, I worked in a busy clinic. It was hectic, with the doctors needing to see back-to-back patients. Before I saw a patient, I did a quick review of their file, which contained their history, other doctors' notes, laboratory records, X-rays and other important tests. A handful of times, the hospital clerk handed me a file, saying the next patient was waiting. On my way to meet the patient, I'd open the file to find nothing in it – no patient name, no past records, no laboratory results. I didn't even know why I was seeing the patient!

I would get so mad that I would confront the clerk, saying, 'There's nothing in this file. How do you expect me to do my work? You need to do yours!'

The clerk would apologise then hurriedly assemble the file. Even after I'd seen the patient, my level of annoyance would still be high because I couldn't imagine why people didn't do their work properly. There was a degree of self-righteousness as well – I was right and they were wrong. They needed to follow procedures or they could ship out.

Funnily, in the beginning, I had a similar attitude towards mindfulness of the breath meditation. I learned it at the local Buddhist centre and thought that their way was the only way of doing it. Then, I attended a Buddhist meditation retreat organised by monks from the Thai Forest Tradition.

The monk started by talking about relaxing the body and focusing on sensations. This went on for a few minutes and, in my mind, I was already becoming restless. This was different from how I had learned to do mindfulness meditation. I decided I'd better ignore this monk and do my own thing and focus on my breathing. Why should I bother with the body? This monk doesn't know what he's talking about. Then it dawned on me that this monk had been meditating for more than 30 years, while I had been doing it for a few months. I realised it was possible that there might be other techniques for practising mindfulness meditation.

It was more than 10 years after I became acquainted with Buddhist meditation and philosophy that I encountered the teaching on 'no fixed views'. I knew that people could get addicted or attached to objects, pleasures, sensations, alcohol and drugs, but I didn't realise that we could get addicted to our own ideas, beliefs and routines. When I heard this, it was a complete revelation to me. A light-bulb moment!

Our addictions can also take the form of achievements.

Luke

My doctor friend Luke has done exceedingly well in terms of studies, sports and music. He was top of his medical school class. He achieved distinction in his cello examinations and is a sought-after soloist. He has played high-level tennis and won competitions in his grade.

I told him how many of us look at him with awe and a tinge of envy. Astonishingly, he looked sad when I said that. He said that he had to be top of his class because being second was not good enough. He had to be the best cello player because, again, being second was not acceptable. It was the same with tennis.

Despite what he had achieved, he had a perpetual feeling of 'lack'. Something was missing.

Growing up, his mother had been controlling and constantly nagged him, which also fed this feeling that he had to be the best at whatever he did. If the neighbour's son John studied and did well in Spanish, Luke had to enrol in a Spanish course too, so that he could eventually achieve a higher mark than John. Luke's life was an endless treadmill of trying to achieve and win. He and his mother are both addicted to achievements and being the best.

· ·

Hack 43: Once you identify your addictions, be open to changing your relationship with them and holding them lightly.

· ·

Self-reflection

Addictions can take the form of activities, routines, preferences, objects, people, beliefs and opinions that you are attached to and hold tightly.

What are your addictions?

Are you open to changing your relationship with them in order to live simply?

Instead of grasping, can you hold on to them lightly?

Will you be okay if, later, you are able to let go?

Addictions overpromise and underdeliver

Only when we seriously look at our addictions will we see the glaring truth that they all overpromise and underdeliver.

It is true that the extra scoop of salted caramel ice cream will make me happy – but only for a short amount of time. Then, I'll crave another scoop, then my stomach and blood sugar will suffer.

One of the biggest drivers for craving and addiction is an internal sense that something is lacking. We are missing on something. Nowadays, we call it FOMO, fear of missing out. Add to that the constant feeling of lack the almighty advertising machine creates in us by telling us that we will be happier, prettier and more complete if we purchase *the* bag, *the* flashy car or *the* beauty product.

Over the past few years, targeted advertising in social media and smart algorithms have unconsciously brainwashed us into comparing ourselves to the idealised lives of influencers, thereby fuelling FOMO to degrees never seen before. Addiction, both legal and illegal, is big business! Living simply is the antidote to the plague of addiction. We break free from its shackles and find contentment in holding things lightly.

CHAPTER 13

Unshackling from our addictions

How can we unshackle ourselves from addiction? Accepting we have these various addictions is the first step. Having the desire to be loosened from their grips is the second step. Employing various proven strategies to become de-addicted is the third step towards our goal of holding things lightly and letting go.

Me telling you that addictions do not satisfy is just conceptual knowledge. Only when you discover it from your own experience will the wisdom of renunciation make sense.

Given the nature of our minds, which are always grasping, habituating and constantly looking for the next hit, we cannot delude ourselves that we will be truly satisfied.

This craving is driven by a sense of not having, that something is missing, something is just not right. We are deluded in thinking that giving in or satisfying it will satiate us for good. The sense of not having is a bottomless vortex that we have evolved with.

. . . .

Hack 44: Unshackling ourselves from the seductive chains of our addictions requires brutally honest self-reflection.

. . . .

Self-reflection

After giving in to your cravings, grasping and desires, have you ever felt completely satisfied?

Did the feeling of incompleteness and lack go away for good?

For most of us, these periods of feeling complete are few and far between.

Step 1: Accepting our addictions

Having addictions and attachments is all part of being a normal human being. Do not feel bad! There is nothing wrong with you. All of us are afflicted with addictions and attachments. Some of these may be mild afflictions while a few are serious and life-threatening.

Our brain wiring and conditioning are the cause. Even Ajahn Chah, one of Thailand's most revered Buddhist teachers, told his monks, 'Being a monk is about letting go, but being unable to do so 90 per cent of the time.'

Knowing and accepting our attachments, even though we are still bound to them, is the start. Only after getting to know these shackles, will we be able to loosen them.

Step 2: Wanting to be loosened from the grip of addiction

Remembering that these very addictions cause us suffering, especially when they are not fulfilled or given in to, is already a motivation to work on them. Wouldn't it be nice and freeing if you could become content with three pairs of shoes instead of having 50? How light would you feel if you were not as controlling over your spouse and children? Can you imagine not having the urge to check your phone every few minutes?

Our tendency to grasp and cling is best illustrated by the monkey trap. The story goes that in India, farmers used to catch monkeys by creating a trap using coconuts. They carved out the coconut, put a banana or something delicious inside and tied it to a tree. A monkey would then come along and attempt to take the banana by sliding its hand into the small hole. The hole was so small that the monkey was unable to withdraw its hand while still holding the banana. Only when a monkey released the banana could it free itself. Greedy monkeys, like many of us, kept holding on and grasping the banana to their detriment.

Practise responding to addiction

When you are in grasping mode for an object, experience, person or situation, notice the tension created in your mind and the body.

Breathe through it.

Be at peace with the craving.

Remind yourself at this very moment, 'I am okay, I am enough, I am adequate.'

> Eventually, craving subsides, giving way to a feeling of release, calm and peace.
>
> Holding our addictions lightly, not grasping on to them, allows us to remove from our minds all the useless things we thought would make us feel happy.

Step 3: Strategies for non-addiction to objects

Hack 45: Know the difference between needs and wants.

Clarissa de la Paz and Monique Leonardo Carlos, authors on financial literacy for children, emphasise that young people should develop the skill of knowing what they need versus what they want. They say needs are 'have to have' and wants are 'nice to have'. Children, and dare I say many adults, cannot differentiate needs versus wants.

Most of the time, I have a good grasp of needs versus wants, until I am let loose at Costco or in an outlet mall. In the past, I have let my cravings run wild and have justified my over-shopping with the mantra 'I work hard, and I don't do drugs'. The depth of these cravings was brought home to me recently when I decluttered my closet and found several pairs of designer pants I'd bought 10 years ago – still with their tags on.

After living simply as a monk with very few possessions, I have become a bit more discerning with needs versus wants. When I am in a mall, I ask myself, 'Do I really need that heavily discounted hoodie?'

More than 90 per cent of the time, the answer is, 'It would be nice to have but I don't really need it.'

On the odd occasion that I give in, I make sure I discard at least one item from my closet when I get home.

Rewind and fast-forward

Another trick I employ to disempower the grip of desire is the rewind and fast-forward technique. This strategy has saved me thousands of dollars through the years.

When I catch myself drooling over a fancy watch, I ask myself the rewind question: 'Tony, before you saw that watch in the shop window, did you actually think you needed a Rolex?' The answer is often no.

Then I ask the fast-forward question: 'Imagine buying that Rolex watch. Does it make you feel really good and does that good feeling last?' Often, the answer is no.

The rewind and fast-forward technique takes the gloss off the excitement brought on by the mental process of desiring. It quickly brings me back down to earth.

I have that

Another strategy I employ when in shopping mode is to tell myself, 'Oh, I have that!'

If I see items in a shop or a mall, for example, a nice set of kitchen knives, I tell myself, 'I have functional knives.' And while walking down the TV aisle, I say, 'I have a good TV.'

After a while, going to the shops becomes a boring experience because I see many things that I already have. By doing this, window-shopping can become a chore, or it can become an exercise of gratitude for the many things I already have.

Buying to benefit

One technique I have occasionally used when I am aware that I have a strong urge to go shopping, is to acknowledge the feeling of wanting to shop. Instead of buying something for myself, I buy something that will benefit others. It has made shopping more exciting and fulfilling. Buying to benefit others can be a fun exercise.

A friend of mine enjoys shopping for cartons of coconut drink. I asked her what the excitement was all about. She shared her practice of giving beggars coconut drinks, which they appreciate. I adapted her strategy and I get excited buying protein bars. I learned from one homeless youth that protein bars are good if one is homeless as they are easy to carry, not messy to eat and have a long shelf life. When someone knocks on my car window and asks for money, I ask if they would like a protein bar. So far, everyone has been appreciative.

Decluttering exercise

One approach to changing our relationship to material objects is decluttering. Go through your cupboards, cabinets, pantry, storage spaces and garage.

Have a clear and realistic goal.

Take out items that you have not used or touched the past two years.

Remove any items that are redundant.

Sort the items into several categories like 'keep', 'donate', 'sell' and 'discard'.

Focus on how grateful you are to have had the opportunity to buy and collect so many objects.

Accept that it is now time for others to benefit from them.

Japanese decluttering superstar Marie Kondo's approach is to keep only the items that spark joy, happiness or positive emotions.

After I declutter, I use the 'one in one out', or even 'one in two out' policy. Every time I buy a new shirt, one or two old shirts go into the donate box.

The power of gratitude and contentment

The main engine driving the desire to acquire and accumulate is the persistent feeling of lack or missing out. Though this feeling of lack may have survival value, it can also lead to unhealthy addictions and a compulsion to continually chase after the positive feeling states we get from eating, shopping, substances, gaming, gambling … basically anything that makes us feel good.

An effective antidote to this chronic state of perceived lack is developing an attitude of gratitude and contentment. If we feel content and grateful with what we have, we deprive the engine of desire its valuable fuel. Even if they have just basic possessions, a person who is grateful and content is richer than a billionaire who constantly craves. The Buddha said that 'contentment is the greatest wealth'.

For a research project, I interviewed patients who were close to death. Many of them talked about simplifying their lives and being content with simple joys. One of them, who had been the CEO of a large farming equipment company, talked about feeling thankful for being able to catch up with friends and see his family. He said that, in a weird way, he was thankful for having cancer and being close to death because only then had he realised that many of his possessions did not mean much. Only with stage four cancer did he appreciate the people who loved him. The same gentleman told me that he experienced great joy when the morning sunlight caressed his legs.

Another research participant told me that she had ignored her body for most of her life. Only after finding out that she would die soon did she become appreciative of every breath that she was able to take.

. . . .

Hack 46: Gratitude is an antidote to our constant grasping.

. . . .

We don't have to wait for a terminal diagnosis or for some disaster to strike to develop gratitude and feel contentment in our lives. Since we are creatures of habit, we cannot simply switch our greedy minds from being whiny and whingy to being grateful. If we want to enhance gratitude, an antidote to materialism and the nagging feeling of lack, there are well-researched approaches that can help us cultivate it.

There are several studies that show enhancing gratitude might be linked to less materialism or greed. Better still, there are proven techniques to enhance gratitude that have been studied through the years.

Writing a gratitude journal is one of the most studied gratitude interventions. There are different types of instructions on how to do this, but most of them involve writing in a diary. Writing things down is an important component of the exercise, as the positive effects are stronger when the physical action of writing occurs than when you just think about things. The process of writing a journal helps get you into the habit of having gratitude.

Gratitude exercise

Set a regular time when you will write in your diary.

At least three times a week, write three to five things you are grateful for.

You can be thankful for people, events or situations.

You can write about things that might seem trivial: 'Someone smiled and opened the door for me at the office.'

You can write about things that are significant: 'I have been having stomach aches again, but my cancer screening test was negative!'

Try to be as specific and descriptive as possible.

View good situations or events as gifts instead of things you feel you deserve.

You can repeat things in your diary, but try to look for different reasons why you are grateful for them. For example: 'I am thankful for my children because today they showed how much they appreciated me as a mother.' Then another diary entry might be: 'I am thankful for my children because they were on time today, which helped us avoid the traffic.'

For several years, I wrote in a gratitude diary. Even now, when I read what I've written in them, I will chuckle and feel good that I've had so many positive events in my life. Were it not for my diary, I would have forgotten hundreds if not thousands of little and big events for which I can be grateful.

Even though I no longer write in my gratitude diary regularly, I am still conscious of the innumerable things for which I am grateful.

When I wake up in the morning, I am grateful to have another day.

When I turn on the shower, I am grateful for the luxury of having clean, warm water at my fingertips. Many people in the world must walk for miles just to have contaminated water.

When it rains, even if it's a bit of an inconvenience, I try to be thankful for the water it brings. Our dams need filling up occasionally.

When it is sunny, I try to be thankful for the warmth, light and joy it brings.

When I mindfully breathe, I am thankful that I can still breathe. I am thankful for the Buddha and his students who have transmitted his priceless gift of mindfulness of the breath to me and millions of other students across 2600 years.

Grateful breathing exercise

Without the breath, we can only survive for a few minutes.

Acknowledge your breath, by breathing in and breathing out, then quietly saying, 'I am thankful for my breath.'

I was enjoying the view in a tourist spot high above the mountains of Burma. There were not many foreign tourists, so I stood out. Five young monks, in their teens, approached me and asked if they could practise their English with me. I enthusiastically agreed.

It turned out to be a complicated process as only one of them spoke understandable English. The rest attempted to say a word or two followed by a lot of sign language and giggling.

I never got the name of the conversant one, but I will never forget him. He was smiley and looked me in the eye when we talked.

I asked him how his life was as a monk. He said he was happy.

As a cynical psychiatrist, I needed to dig deeper. I asked him if there are things he wanted to change in his life. He said no.

I asked if he missed hanging out with females. He said, 'Not really, I made a choice to be a monk and as a monk I cannot hang out with women.'

I asked about his phone, which was an old smartphone with a cracked screen. He said, 'It's good.'

I asked if he wanted a new phone. He said, 'It's okay, it still works.'

I asked if there was Wi-Fi at his monastery. He said, 'There isn't, but that's okay.'

I thought about teenagers in other parts of the world. If I'd asked them what they wanted, they would have come up with a huge list of things, people and experiences that they thought would make them happy.

I asked him if he was sure there was nothing he wanted to be different in his life. He said, 'Oh yes, there is something I want.'

Finally! He *was* a normal teenager with normal cravings and desires ...

He said, 'I wish I could get up earlier in the morning so that I don't miss meditation. But otherwise, I am content.'

Holding views lightly in the palms of our hands

There is no question that we will always have views. We are a thinking species and having views is critical to survival. We have views from how to hold a knife and fork to how governments should be run – but there are different ways we can hold on to our views. We can grasp on to them as if our lives depend on them, or we can hold them lightly in the palms of our hands. We do not have to be addicted to them.

In several of his teachings, the Buddha talked about not having fixed views. In one of his most famous teachings, the Mettā Sutta (teachings on loving kindness), he said that not holding to fixed views leads to the highest happiness.

In another teaching, called the Simile of the Raft, he instructed his followers to see his teachings as a raft that should be abandoned once the shore of true happiness is reached. In essence, he was telling his students not to be attached to his teachings!

I have never known any famous teacher who has told their students to eventually discard their teachings. The Buddha was incredibly ego-less when he gave this teaching – a perfect example of not having fixed views.

Self-reflection

Do you have ideas, beliefs and routines that you are attached to? (These can range from the best way to stack the dishwasher, right through to religious and political beliefs.)

If someone has a differing perspective, do you think of them as wrong or ignorant?

Are you open to changing your ideas, beliefs and routines if you are presented with better alternatives?

If you answered yes to the first two questions and no to the third, you are addicted and you will need a bit of unshackling from your chains of self-righteousness if you want to be happy.

At a Spanish-language course in Salamanca, our teacher was an older lady who was very particular about pronunciation and grammar. She was what many of the students considered to be 'old school'.

We were discussing Spanish cuisine and the topic was making paella. The students were expected to recite the various ingredients, which included rice, saffron, fish, mussels and broth.

She then called me and asked in Spanish, 'Antonio! What are other paella ingredients?'

I proudly said, 'Chorizo!'

She glared at me and shouted, 'Nunca!' (Never).

Then she gave a sermon about how chorizo is a mistake before asking me where I had eaten paella with chorizo.

I told her that a lot of places in the Philippines, the US and New Zealand use chorizo in paella. I then confessed that I also put chorizo in my paella.

This made her even more angry. I began to wonder whether her traditional, fixed views on paella might cause her some medical harm.

At a societal level, extreme fixed views have caused incalculable harm and destruction. The Nazis were addicted to the concept of the superiority of the Aryan race and the inferiority of other races and groups. Millions of people were unjustly targeted and persecuted based on these fixed, erroneous views that have no scientific basis.

These views resulted in the deaths of millions of people, including Jews, Poles, Slavs, Romani, gay and disabled people, as well as many thousands of people who disagreed with the Nazis politically.

Not so long after the Holocaust, Pol Pot and the Khmer Rouge were fixed on the idea of a utopian and classless society, which resulted in the genocide of close to two million Cambodians, who were perceived as threats to their goals. These included intellectuals, professionals, those who worked with the previous government and people who simply wore glasses. The dream of a classless society became a nightmare for millions of Cambodians.

More recently, religious fundamentalism and political extremism have been causing chaos in the Middle East, Europe and the US. Groups of humans will insist that their view is the only correct one and everyone else is wrong.

Are we wired to have fixed views?

Having fixed views seems to be a part of being human. It is even possible that we are wired to be inclined to be attached to views.

During ancient times, when you saw someone who looked different or unusual, they had to be treated with suspicion, in case they were hostile. Perhaps they had plans to invade, steal food or enslave your people. Thinking flexibly – perhaps the person is just lost – had the potential to be costly. Instead, having a fixed view that we should be careful of people who are different to ourselves had survival value.

We also like our thoughts and beliefs to be neat and tidy. We like them to be consistent and coherent. We also develop emotional attachment to what we believe in.

For example, if I do not believe in climate change, talking to someone who believes in it and argues for its existence causes intellectual discomfort. It is the same with religious or political beliefs. When we encounter someone with a differing opinion, our stomach might churn and we might feel tense. If this happens, it's because our views have become part of who we are and anyone who has another perspective is seen as a threat.

Birds of a feather flock together

We tend to surround ourselves with people who hold similar views, which further reinforces our beliefs. Fixed views bind people together and provide a form of social glue. Again, this has survival value as, in ancient times, we needed to be part of a group in order to survive.

At a meeting of doctors, nurses, psychologists and social workers, we had to discuss a complicated psychiatric patient who was not getting better despite various interventions. The discussion became fiery a few times as people had strong but differing ideas about what needed to be done.

A few times I acknowledged why people felt a certain way but also reminded them to be open to other people's suggestions. When the meeting ended, a more senior doctor approached me and asked, 'Why are you so agreeable?' He went on to say he found me being open to different ideas offensive and undoctor-like. I just smiled and let it go – he was displaying a fixed view that I did not agree with.

How can we hold our views lightly instead of grasping on to them?

To soften fixed views, remember impermanence – everything changes.

If I honestly examine the fixed views that I have held through the years – views on religion, how to diagnose and manage certain disorders, how to play certain musical pieces, and how people should behave in certain situations – they have all changed. What I thought were fixed views that I would never compromise on have all eventually softened.

For decades, I adhered to the strict rule that the audience should be 100 per cent quiet at classical music concerts. Any sound from phones, rustling of programmes or even loud breathing annoyed the hell out of me. I'd give people dagger looks and I've even told people to shut up. But in the history of classical music, it wasn't always like this. In the nineteenth century, many music halls didn't observe the rule of absolute quiet.

Through the years, I have softened my stance, though I still highly value the importance of following the quiet protocol. Nowadays, I still remind people to be quiet if they can, but I do not get red-hot angry or self-righteous about it.

Whenever we hold fixed views, from science, to religion, to politics, to how to roast a chicken, be on the lookout for evidence to the contrary.

I am not espousing discarding all our views. However, a less stressful alternative is to hold them lightly. Recognise that this is how we view things for now, but our minds can and will change. Also, advances in human knowledge might prove us wrong.

Be genuinely curious, without judgment, as to how others view the world

Another way to soften our fixed views is to be genuinely curious regarding alternative views.

I became quite interested in the conflict in the Middle East while visiting Israel. I had my fixed Buddhist view that the solution to the crisis was for all parties to truly understand how each other live – their fears, their joys, their hopes and their suffering.

I was fixed in this view of how the conflict could be resolved, even though I had never studied Middle Eastern politics or history in depth. There was also a degree of self-righteousness about my 'enlightened' view.

At the Western Wall in Jerusalem I met an American who lived in the city and whose perspective on Palestinians shook my core. He was 100 per cent sure that Palestinians were the root cause of the problems in the Middle East: 'All Palestinians cannot be trusted.'

His views on how Palestinians should be treated made me sick. But at the same time, I was curious as to how he'd come to this conclusion. I became curious about him as a person rather than focusing on his extreme views or telling him that he was 200 per cent wrong. Instead of getting angry at him, I felt sad that that was how he viewed the 'other' group.

On the same day, I was able to chat with a falafel shop owner, a young Palestinian man whose family had lived and worked in the same shop-house in Old City, Jerusalem for many years. He had fixed views on how to solve the conflict and, as expected, his solution made me feel unwell too.

Instead of judging him as wrong and unenlightened, I was curious as to how he'd come up with his ideas and how his family had suffered in the past few decades. Even so, it was hard for me to be genuinely curious and not judge people who had totally different views to mine.

There have been times when I've been talking to people whose views are radically different from mine that I've had the urge to smack them in the head in the hope of waking them up from their unenlightened slumber. Isn't that a perfect example of me having fixed views?

After talking to different people in Israel, secular and ultra-Orthodox Jews, Palestinian Muslims and Palestinian Christians, I can admit that I don't know what the best way forward is. I still believe that compassion is the only way but how to get there is so complicated. I still have my views, but they are not so fixed for me to claim the higher ground and insist my views are correct – that would be unenlightened and self-righteous.

Kyle

Kyle is a staunch campaigner for a New Zealand political party. One day, he described to me how his views have evolved through the years.

When he was younger, he categorised everything – people, concepts, beliefs and behaviours – as either right or wrong. As such, he mentally assigned them to the 'right' box or the 'wrong' box.

Later in his life, he added a 'different' box, which was where he could put the things he didn't see as being either right or wrong. As he has gained more wisdom, worked and met people from various cultures and ethnic groups, his 'different' box grew and is now the biggest of the three, while the 'right' and 'wrong' boxes have shrunk.

Chicken or duck

One of the teachers who got me interested in the Buddha's teachings was Ajahn Brahm. He is an English monk, and has a PhD in physics from Cambridge University. Aside from being hilarious and irreverent, he often shares anecdotes and metaphors that really stick in the mind. One of these, which is relevant to the concept of not having fixed ideas, is the chicken or duck story.

A newlywed couple went for a stroll in the woods after dinner. They were enjoying each other's company until they heard a sound: *Quack, quack.*

The wife said, 'That's a chicken.'

The husband said, 'No, darling, that's a duck.'

'It's definitely a chicken,' the wife insisted.

The husband said, 'No, dear, chickens go *cock-a-doodle-doo* while ducks go *quack, quack.*'

Whatever the creature was, it continued to quack.

The wife said, 'See! It's a chicken.'

Getting angrier, the husband said, 'You are such an idiot! How can you call that a chicken? It's a blooming duck ... D ... U ... C... K. DUCK, the bird that swims and has webbed feet!'

The wife started to cry, but still insisted, 'It's a chicken.'

The husband saw her tears. His face softened. He remembered how much he loved her. He looked at the wife and said, 'Yes, darling, you might be right ... it's a chicken.'

The husband realised that it was not important whether it was a chicken or a duck. They were just words or views. What was important was their love for each other and their beautiful evening walks.

How many times have we sacrificed precious friendships and relationships over our fixed views on politics, or how things should be done, or how people should behave? I know of a couple who separated because they couldn't stand each other's preferred toothpaste brand.

We get so hung up with what we think is correct and forget that relationships are more important. We do not have to give up our views, but we can hold them lightly and make space for others.

CHAPTER 14

Kindness and compassion

I grew up in a single-parent household with seven siblings. I was number eight. My mother worked so hard, with the help of my grandmother, to make sure that we were well fed and attended good schools. I cannot remember my mother buying things for herself. Her sole focus was her eight children.

She had a pair of small earrings with green jade in a setting with a thin strand of gold. They were her most valuable possession. I saw that pair of earrings go in and out of pawnshops at the beginning of each school year, so we could have extra money to buy books and school supplies.

She worked as a public-school teacher in a faraway school, and, after work, she had to cook and sort out her children. In addition to providing for her children, she unwaveringly helped relatives who were poorer than us. A part of me was annoyed by her generosity, as I would have preferred all her meagre earnings to go to us, her children. She never complained or expressed resentment about her hard life. My mother is one of my role models for kindness and compassion.

In New Zealand, when the Covid pandemic started, Prime Minister Jacinda Ardern became world famous for the promotion of kindness and compassion. In addition to reminding every New Zealander to isolate and social distance, she ended her speeches with the words 'Be kind'. Public safety reminders, digital road signs and supermarkets shared the message 'Be kind'. As the population was anxious and distressed, this was a timely and appropriate reminder to think of others and not just ourselves.

This message of kindness and compassion was certainly not a new one. The world's great religious and philosophical traditions espouse and sometimes even command love, kindness and compassion.

Jesus Christ's teaching on kindness is considered one of Christianity's main commandments. Prophet Muhammad talked about kindness as a mark of faith, and also said whoever is not kind has no faith. Kindness, charity and non-violence are key teachings in Buddhism, Christianity, Islam, Hinduism, Sikhism, Judaism, Taoism, Confucianism and the Bahá'í faith.

Sadly, despite these teachings on kindness, compassion and non-violence, humanity's behaviour has remained disheartteningly consistent throughout history. From ancient times to the present century, humans have repeatedly displayed a tendency towards cruelty, greed and mistreatment. Hitler, Stalin, Pol Pot and Chairman Mao are just a few of the many world leaders who have deliberately tortured and killed millions of humans who they considered to be their enemies.

Some might say that these world leaders committed these crimes because they were not religious and did not practise their faiths properly. However, even religious leaders, including those of faiths that advocate kindness, have justified subjugation, slavery and massacres in the name of their religion.

Only recently did the leaders of the Catholic church, Pope John Paul II and Pope Francis, publicly acknowledge and ask for forgiveness for a millennium of the church's sins in the form of violence against non-believers.

Talking about kindness, even making it a religious commandment, doesn't seem effective in making people kind. You can remind (or threaten!) your children to be kind until the cows come home, but they will still end up smacking each other on a regular basis. Talking about and teaching kindness, love and compassion is not enough to make any of us behave kindly and compassionately towards each other.

What does it really mean to be kind and compassionate?

Many confuse these terms and think that they are the same. Though both belong to what, in psychology, we call prosocial mental states – mind states that are focused on the wellbeing or benefit of others – there are subtle differences between kindness and compassion.

To be kind is to be well-meaning, friendly, considerate, agreeable and generous. Kindness involves treating others the way you would treat your loved ones. The emotional tone associated with a kind act is often that of joy or happiness.

Compassion is a natural step on from kindness. If you want a person who is suffering to experience happiness, compassion – the wish for them to be free of suffering – arises.

Compassion is sensitivity to other beings' suffering coupled with the desire to help them with or alleviate their difficulties. When one is compassionate, it is not unusual for the initial emotions of sadness, sympathy and even discomfort to be triggered by witnessing suffering. With the extra step of desiring to help, a compassionate person feels warm, complete, meaningful and with a sense of purpose.

Feeling warm and purposeful when we engage in acts of kindness and compassion has been studied through the lens of neuroscience. Neuroimaging experiments, or studies involving high-tech pictures of the brain, showed that when subjects are in a compassionate state, the brain regions involved in feeling rewarded, connected and positive all light up. In other words, engaging in compassionate acts or thoughts can make us feel good.

What is the difference between romantic love and kindness and compassion?

Romantic love is a complicated emotional state that can have elements of kindness and compassion in the mix. However, romantic love often involves terms and conditions for the relationship. Genuine kindness and compassion are without conditions.

Romantic love is often associated with warm, exciting and tingly feelings. There is often an expectation that the love will be reciprocated. There is often lust or a sexual component in romantic love.

Romantic love is often conditional on how the other person looks, smells and behaves. If the other person does not reciprocate or behaves differently from what is expected, romantic love dissipates and turns to disinterest or even anger and hate. In other words, romantic love is fickle.

True kindness and compassion are unconditional and independent of feelings. However, for those who are untrained, kindness and compassion are often conditional.

The seeds of compassion

I have always been interested in the phenomena of helping and compassion. I am not sure what made me interested in the topic, but growing up in Manila, I was lucky to witness lots of kind acts. It is possible that being exposed to kindness and compassion early in life has piqued my academic interest in the topic. My mother's unremitting selflessness to care for her children modelled to me and my siblings the importance of unconditional compassion. Without her compassion, we would not have survived.

When I was studying at the University of the Philippines medical school in the late 1980s, we had many patients who could not afford basic medications, including life-saving antibiotics. At that time, medical students had to be creative when it came to sourcing these medications to give to their patients. My go-to resource was my eldest sister.

At that time, she was working for a finance company and earning modestly. I cannot remember the number of times I rang her in desperation because I had paediatric patients who would have died without antibiotics.

Without hesitation, she transferred money to my account, no questions asked, just to help my patients. Though organising this funding was stressful, I can still remember the exhilaration and incredible joy I felt when the funds came through and my patients got their treatment.

Having worked as a doctor for more than 30 years, I often reflect on my medical practice and think about the aspects of medicine that have given me meaning and joy, and the activities I've been involved with that have fuelled me to continue working in this exhausting profession. The main things that stand out are acts of compassion, particularly when I have understood my patients and helped them in their suffering. Reflecting on these moments has made all the hard slog worthwhile.

Burnout is prevalent among senior doctors nowadays with at least 50 per cent of us reporting excessive fatigue and burnout. One way I have avoided burnout is by reflecting on compassion and the benefit it has brought other people.

I have consciously collected and catalogued comments, letters and emails from grateful patients. Reading them occasionally, particularly when the going gets tough, reminds me that listening to patients, acknowledging their suffering and doing my best to give them a better life is the heart and soul of my practice of medicine.

Compassion satisfaction

The pleasure one experiences from caring is known as compassion satisfaction. I am sure my mother felt good helping our poor relations even though she didn't have much to give.

There has been some research on compassion satisfaction involving those who work in healthcare. Not surprisingly, those with high levels of compassion satisfaction appear to be less burnt out by their work compared to those with low compassion satisfaction. It appears that experiencing the pleasure from kindness and compassion helps protect us from negative emotions, distress and burnout.

Compassion satisfaction exercise:

Close your eyes, feel your breath coming in and out. Settle in the calm of your breath.

Recall an incident when you showed kindness and compassion to someone else, and the recipient thanked you for it.

Picture the face of the person, the smile and the warmth they exuded.

Recall the emotion you felt. Savour these feelings of warmth and connection.

Remember that acts of compassion benefit not just others but yourself as well.

Silently tell yourself, 'Compassion benefits not just others but me as well.'

Gently open your eyes and carry this sense of compassion satisfaction with you.

The formal study of compassion

As an academic psychiatrist at the University of Auckland medical school, I was expected to pursue a PhD in a topic that interested me. Over the years, my various bosses have encouraged me to study, reminding me of how important it would be for academic promotion and the prestige of the academic department. For more than 10 years, I was unable to find a clinical topic that interested me enough to want to spend years researching it. That was until I stumbled on the idea of compassion as a research topic – more specifically – how to make doctors more compassionate.

My PhD research focused on compassion among medical doctors, students and nurses. One of the remarkable findings of our various studies was that compassion is not easy. Even if doctors and nurses want to be compassionate, as compassion is the heart of our profession, many of us are burnt out and do not have much compassion left to give.

Our research group identified various factors that block compassion. We found that the negative emotional states of the doctor, difficult patients and families and unhealthy work situations all hamper compassion. Though our research has not involved a non-clinical population, my guess is that our findings that compassion is not that easy applies to everyone.

Kindness and compassion are not easy

Even though we want to be kind and compassionate and we know that being kind and compassionate is vital in human relationships, practising it is not easy. Think about the countless times when you've had unkind and uncompassionate thoughts and urges towards other people, be they ones you love, like or can't stand.

Daniel Batson, a well-renowned American social psychologist, performed an enlightening study looking at compassionate behaviour among Princeton University theology students. The experiment examined the effects of external stress on compassionate behaviours.

In the study, Princeton seminarians were tasked with preparing a talk on the parable of the Good Samaritan, a biblical story depicting compassion to strangers. One group of seminarians was given sufficient time to prepare the sermon while another group was pressured to prepare it in just a few minutes.

The seminarians were instructed to deliver the sermon in another building on campus. On the way to the other building, they encountered a shabbily dressed, slumped stranger on the road. Those who were in a hurry ignored the man while members of the more relaxed group were more willing to help. It didn't matter that the students were preparing to give a sermon on compassion to strangers, as their sense of urgency diminished the likelihood of helping others. It appears that when we are stressed, compassion goes out the window.

My grandmother, who we fondly called Lola, which means granny in my native language, Filipino, was very religious. She was a daily churchgoer, prayed the rosary several times a day, spent at least an hour saying her prayers in the morning before church and wore her white Virgin Mary devotional dress with a blue sash daily at mass. Our house was full of religious icons, with one almost life-sized image of the Blessed Virgin Mary.

This massive statue of Mary had several sets of vestments, gold pendants with diamonds, a crown of gold with rubies, emeralds and diamonds, and rosary beads made of gold. Such was the devotion of my Lola. We even had a proper chapel with a massive altar in the middle of our house where, several times a year, we held big religious festivals, some of which lasted for days.

Though she was loving of her grandchildren, Lola could have the sharpest tongue and the meanest attitude when stressed. She scared the hell out of us when she was in a grumpy mood. She would slam her massive leather purse on the table, accompanied by a loud curse in Spanish. Her religious fervour, kindness and Christian compassion evaporated when she was in a foul mood.

In-group kindness

When you hear that a loved one or someone in your close circle has been in a car crash, you instantly feel sad, shocked, upset and sympathetic. Not surprisingly, you will ask how you can help, send flowers or even raise funds for the family.

Would you feel the same shock and sadness if the person in the accident was someone you didn't know? How willing would you be to donate even a dollar to someone you didn't feel any connection with?

Have you noticed that TV advertisements asking for donations for children use pictures of kids from various ethnic groups? Advertisers know that a potential donor is more likely to feel connected to a child who looks like them.

When Russia invaded Ukraine in 2022, there was huge outrage in the west. However, the ongoing famine in Yemen, which has endangered the lives of 20 million people, and horrific flooding in Pakistan, which covered a third of the country, have barely been mentioned on the news or social media in the western world.

We want to see ourselves as kind, but we are selective about who we are kind to. We tend to be kind and compassionate only to those who we believe are in our clan or clique. In psychology, we call it our 'in-group'.

Why is our kindness and compassion not naturally universal?

If we genuinely want to become kinder and more caring, it helps to understand the human mind.

Mammals and birds have evolved to take care of and protect our own kin. Young mammals and birds will not survive without caring mothers and, occasionally, fathers. Young mammals and birds are vulnerable to predators and will die without sufficient food and water. Other animals, like reptiles, fish and amphibians, can survive on their own without parental care. A baby snake can just slither off into the wild and survive, whereas a human baby needs many years of constant care and attention to survive.

It is hypothesised that this caring behaviour of parents, particularly mothers, is where kindness and compassion come from. Without a mother's kindness and compassion to their vulnerable offspring, the child will die. If the children die, the species will not survive. Kindness and compassion are crucial for the survival of humans and other mammals.

Even though kindness and caring behaviours are essential for the species to continue, they are not offered to everyone. Kindness and compassion are often conditional, which means they are offered depending on or conditional to certain situations. In other words, we are not always kind and compassionate to everyone.

Humans are more likely to help relatives or genetically related members of a group rather than non-relatives. This tendency to be kinder to family members has also been seen in primates, where observations suggest that, after a chimpanzee is defeated in a brutal fight, consolation is mainly offered by the loser's relatives and friends. There is truth to the saying 'blood is thicker than water'.

Humans also tend to be more compassionate towards others with whom they feel connected or those who share their values or interests. We tend to be kinder to those who are like us. Bottom line, we are not naturally kind or caring to everyone.

We are selective, consciously or unconsciously, as to who we want to help. If someone in need is in our in-group, it is likely that they will be helped. If they are outside our circle, we are less likely to help.

The flipside of our evolved tendency to be kind to those in our clan is that we are less kind or sometimes do not have positive feelings towards other people outside our perceived group.

People outside the perceived group might be those who belong to another ethnic group, socioeconomic class, religion or political persuasion. It is not unusual for humans to have thoughts of harming people who are not like them. More than just thoughts and impulses, some even deliberately persecute, discriminate and annihilate those who are outside their clan.

$\cdot \cdot \cdot \cdot \cdot \cdot \cdot \cdot \cdot \cdot \cdot \cdot \cdot \cdot \cdot \cdot \cdot \cdot \cdot \cdot \cdot \cdot \cdot \cdot \cdot \cdot \cdot \cdot \cdot \cdot \cdot \cdot \cdot \cdot \cdot \cdot \cdot \cdot$

Hack 47: Treat everyone you meet as a friend.

$\cdot \cdot \cdot \cdot \cdot \cdot \cdot \cdot \cdot \cdot \cdot \cdot \cdot \cdot \cdot \cdot \cdot \cdot \cdot \cdot \cdot \cdot \cdot \cdot \cdot \cdot \cdot \cdot \cdot \cdot \cdot \cdot \cdot \cdot \cdot \cdot \cdot \cdot$

In Buddhism, we are encouraged to self-reflect and examine our own conditioning, biases and prejudices. We learn to acknowledge that we have built-in conditioned biases and prejudices, as they are part of being human. Our various biological and psychological conditionings are not bad or evil, they are just part of an evolved human brain. This conditioned set of biases and prejudices are influenced by genetics, childhood experiences, education, relationships, advertising, social media and also religious and political propaganda.

One such form of conditioning is our clique mentality. We classify people as belonging or not belonging to our clan. Since this mentality often determines who we are kind or compassionate to, broadening the boundaries to expand who we see as part of our circle is an effective way to increase compassion.

When I was a boy in Manila, society was composed mainly of Filipinos and some Filipino-Chinese as a minority. When I misbehaved, my grandmother warned me that the dark men with bushy beards – a very small group of foreign traders living in my neighbourhood – would pick me up, put me inside a sack and sell me at the market. I feared these foreign, tall, dark men in long robes throughout my childhood.

My conditioning was a classic example of people outside the in-group stereotyped as outcasts and even as bogeymen. Later, in high school, I became friends with the children of these traders, and they were not that different from us, except for their spicy food.

One way to expand our circle is to get to know people from other circles as friends. Becoming friends with people who seem different is a sure-fire way to break prejudices. Suddenly, the scary person who looked different becomes a person you know, can talk to and share food with. To befriend them is to realise that they are not different from us. Those scary, tall, dark men in long robes were no different from my father or older male relatives.

However, we cannot befriend everyone who is different from us. There just isn't enough time to get to know eight billion other people! Fortunately, apart from befriending people from other in-groups, we have the innate capacity to reshape our wiring.

Our brain is neuroplastic and we can learn new ways of thinking. We can reclassify people in our head. We can train our minds to view everyone as exactly like us – as someone in our clan.

The Dalai Lama demonstrates this perfectly when he says, 'I try to treat whoever I meet as an old friend. This gives me a genuine feeling of happiness. This is the practice of compassion.'

There are many anecdotes of the Dalai Lama's spontaneous kindness. When he tours the world giving lectures to thousands of people, he makes sure that he gets to meet the people behind the scenes – the cleaning staff, kitchen hands and support crew. People say that when he talks to strangers he has met for the first time, he gives his full attention to them as if there is no one else who matters.

Of course, he is the Dalai Lama, and he has the capacity to do this. But can we train our minds to be as kind and compassionate as his?

The solution is simple and has been practised for 2600 years, yet it is rarely talked about or even taught in schools. It works so well that if taught to our younger generations, the possibility of global conflict and warfare would diminish.

In Buddhist kindness and compassion training, instead of noticing how different other people are, we train ourselves to look at what is similar between us and the 'other'. The other can be the foreign family who moved in across the street, the homeless person begging outside the supermarket, the person at work who has a paralysed face, or the people in Yemen suffering from the effects of war and poverty. The other can be your annoying relative or your child who constantly disobeys you.

To increase kindness and compassion, try to see others as exactly like you. It is easy to notice how different they are. Instead, focus on what your similarities are.

How can we be similar to other people who we don't even associate with or like? By recognising that regardless of our ethnicity, allegiances, religion, socioeconomic status or political persuasion, *all of us just want the same things.*

We all want to be happy, to be loved, to be safe, to have food, drink and shelter. None of us want stress, anxiety or suffering. We all experience sadness, isolation, loss and death.

CHAPTER 15

Exercising kindness and compassion

Of the various religions and philosophies I have been acquainted with, what attracted me to the teachings of the Buddha is the emphasis on kindness and compassion, not just the theory or admonishments, but the actual *practice*.

While kindness and compassion are not specific to Buddhist philosophy, they are at the heart of being a Buddhist. That might explain why, in the main, Buddhists have not resorted to systematic violence against other religious groups.

However, there have been exceptions. Throughout history, some Buddhist groups have been involved in martial arts training and self-defence. Even worse, some Buddhist monks have been implicated in violence against the Rohingya minority in Burma and against the Tamils in Sri Lanka. However, for the most part, Buddhism has been a pacifist movement, which is against violence or harm towards other beings.

In 2013, I stayed at Pullahari Monastery, a Tibetan Buddhist monastery outside of Kathmandu, in Nepal. One afternoon, I spent time with a Buddhist monk who was in his early twenties.

I was curious about his life as a monk and what his training looked like.

While walking together down one of the monastery corridors, he suddenly stopped. Then he slowly stooped and, with gentleness and extreme care, picked up a ladybug from the floor and put it on his palm. He then walked towards a bush and delicately released the bug. We then carried on talking about his life in the monastery as if nothing had happened.

His Holiness the Dalai Lama has often been quoted as saying, 'My religion is kindness. There is no need for temples; no need for complicated philosophy.'

I have met many Buddhist teachers, monks and nuns who have reminded me that if the Buddha's teachings were to be reduced to just one phrase, it would be: Cause no harm.

When it comes to being kind and compassionate to others, merely recognising that we are all the same is not enough. One can understand this concept intellectually as it makes perfect sense, but merely recognising and understanding concepts is not enough to cause a true change in orientation and behaviour.

The recognition that we are all in the same boat has to go deep into our consciousness. Instead of being very quick to notice how other people are different, our mind can be quick to add that there are also lots of similarities.

In a manner of speaking, we need a software update or even a total operational system change. This is where the rich tradition of Buddhism comes in. Buddhism has various mental practices or meditations that have been around for more than 1000 years that have allowed this radical system upgrade to occur. Two traditional kindness and compassion exercises are mettā, or kindness meditation, and Tonglen meditation.

What did the Buddha say about kindness and compassion?

We do not have exact records of what the Buddha actually said, as his teachings were only written down about 600 years after his death. His teachings are called suttas, and were recorded in Pali, one of the languages in India at that time. In the suttas, the Buddha referred to kindness as mettā and compassion as karuna.

The word mettā often refers to strong and genuine wishing of happiness, wellbeing and peace to other beings. It has an attitude of friendliness, kindness, amiability, benevolence, non-harm and non-violence.

While mettā is the wish for others to be happy and at ease, karuna or compassion is the wish for others to be free from suffering. Both mettā and karuna want the best for others, except that karuna or compassion is more specific to both witnessing suffering and the genuine wish for suffering to be alleviated. Like mettā, karuna brings with it an attitude of respect, inclusivity, non-harm and non-violence.

The Dalai Lama states that compassion is the wish that all beings be free from suffering, and loving kindness is the wish that all may enjoy happiness.

In Buddhist teachings, kindness and compassion are two of the four brahma-viharas, or sublime and excellent abodes where human minds should be dwelling. The other two are sympathetic joy and equanimity. Sympathetic joy is rejoicing in other people's happiness. Equanimity is the unshakeable balance of the mind.

These excellent states of mind can be attained by regular practice of meditation. Some meditation masters, including Ajahn Sumedho, comment that when a practitioner is constantly living in the present moment these mind qualities become automatic.

Mettā Sutta

There is a beautiful sutta by the Buddha called the Mettā Sutta. It describes what mettā or kindness is in several levels. This chant is recited in Buddhist monasteries all over the world. It serves as a reminder of what kindness is and how it is to be practised.

The Mettā Sutta details two aspects of kindness. The first aspect describes the personal characteristics and behaviours of someone practising kindness, which includes being upright, straightforward, gentle in speech, humble, content, peaceful and calm. The practitioner of mettā does not deceive or despise others and does not harbour anger or ill-will to anyone.

Second, the Mettā Sutta elaborates a detailed well-wishing to all beings: weak or strong, great or small, seen or unseen, living near or far away – omitting no one. It is an all-inclusive wish for all creatures to live with ease.

This is what should be done
by one who is skilled in goodness,
and who knows the path of peace:
Let them be able and upright,
straightforward and gentle in speech,
humble and not conceited,
contented and easily satisfied,
unburdened with duties and frugal in their ways.
Peaceful and calm and wise and skilful,
not proud or demanding in nature.
Let them not do the slightest thing
that the wise would later reprove.

Wishing: in gladness and in safety,
  may all beings be at ease.
Whatever living beings there may be;
  whether they are weak or strong, omitting none,
the great or the mighty, medium, short or small,
  the seen and the unseen,
those living near and far away,
  those born and to-be-born –
may all beings be at ease!

Let none deceive another,
  or despise any being in any state.
Let none through anger or ill-will
  wish harm upon another.
Even as a mother protects with her life
  her child, her only child,
so with a boundless heart
  should one cherish all living beings.
Radiating kindness over the entire world:
  spreading upwards to the skies,
and downwards to the depths;
  outwards and unbounded,
freed from hatred and ill-will.
  Whether standing or walking, seated or lying down,
free from drowsiness,
  one should sustain this recollection.
This is said to be the sublime abiding.
  By not holding to fixed views,
the pure-hearted one, having clarity of vision,
  being freed from all sense desires,
is not born again into this world.

This chant on kindness is different from other religions' statements of faith as it is not a recitation of what should be believed. Instead, it is a guideline on how to practise kindness in thoughts, speech and action on a day-to-day basis. It is a very detailed exhortation of what it is to be kind, way beyond the usual platitudes of 'be kind' or 'love one another'.

Using the Buddha's wisdom, how, in our current situation, can we develop kindness and compassion? More importantly, what practical things can we do on a regular basis that will make us kinder and more compassionate?

Meditation on kindness and compassion

My first brush with meditation on kindness and compassion occurred in 2004. I enrolled in a six-week basic meditation course at the Auckland Buddhist Centre. The course taught mindfulness meditation first, followed by loving-kindness or mettā meditation. For the first few weeks of the course, I concentrated on mindfulness of the breath. Later, I tried to practise mettā meditation.

The mettā meditation I initially practised consisted of visualisation and imagination. It was very different from mindfulness of the breath meditation. I liked mindfulness of the breath because my mind naturally calmed while practising it. I am not so good with my imagination so, initially, I developed something of a dislike for mettā meditation.

Hack 48: Try mettā meditation for a few months and see if it rewires your mind to be kinder.

The first mettā meditation I did consisted of six stages, with each stage lasting for around three to five minutes – or however long I could tolerate it!

Practise mettā meditation

Sit comfortably with your eyes closed.

Stage one

Imagine someone who cares for you or someone who loves you. It can be a parent, a teacher, a mentor or even a pet.

Imagine this person (or animal) sitting in front of you while saying in your mind: 'May you be free from suffering … may you be safe … may you be happy … may you be at peace.'

It doesn't have to be these exact words but, essentially, you are wishing that the other being not to be in any discomfort and for that person to be at ease.

The phrases should be said slowly and with genuine intent. You do not have to feel anything good. Just say those phrases in your mind for a few minutes.

Stage two

Change the object of your meditation to someone *you* love. It can be a friend, a partner, a relative or anyone for whom you have positive feelings.

Repeat the same phrases for a few minutes: 'May you be free from suffering … may you be safe … may you be happy … may you be at peace.'

Stage three

Imagine yourself sitting in front of you. Some imagine their younger selves in front of them.

Repeat the phrases of kindness and wellbeing: 'May you be free from suffering ... may you be safe ... may you be happy ... may you be at peace.'

Stage four

Imagine a neutral person sitting in front of you. This should be someone whom you don't have any positive or negative feelings for. Perhaps it's a bus driver, a random woman from the laundromat, or someone who makes your coffee.

Repeat the phrases of kindness and wellbeing: 'May you be free from suffering ... may you be safe ... may you be happy ... may you be at peace.'

Stage five

Imagine someone you don't like sitting in front of you. For beginners, I suggest using a person who you find slightly annoying.

Repeat the phrases of kindness and wellbeing: 'May you be free from suffering ... may you be safe ... may you be happy ... may you be at peace.'

When you have good mettā stamina, you can use people who you find really difficult, like politicians or people who have caused you harm.

Stage six

Imagine the whole of humanity and all beings on earth in front of you. (I imagine my loving kindness spreading from my house to the community, to the whole city, country, mountains, oceans, with all the people and all creatures in it.)

Repeat the phrases of kindness and wellbeing: 'May you be free from suffering ... may you be safe ... may you be happy ... may you be at peace.'

Some of you might be inspired by this practice, but initially I was bored stiff and thought it was a load of mumbo jumbo! I wondered how these inane phrases could change me. As a man of science, I thought saying things like that wouldn't change me.

At the same time, I trusted in the meditation process that had been passed down through hundreds of generations of Buddhist practitioners. I told myself I would give this meditation a go, even just for a few months. I also knew that behavioural patterns change following about two months of training.

I did mettā meditation for 10 to 20 minutes a day, most days for two months. Guess what? Nothing changed. So, I said, okay, I'll do it for another month, but that's it.

After about three months of this mumbo-jumbo meditation, I still felt like the same Tony. Then, one morning, I woke up and there were lots of black ants crawling on the kitchen bench.

In the past, I would have gleefully ended their lives with big puffs of fly spray or, if I was feeling a bit maniacal, I'd pound them with my fist. This morning was different. I just saw the ants and did not feel the urge to kill them. Deep inside, I felt that they were just like me, looking for food and wanting to be alive. There was no fear of bad karma or lightning bolts zapping me. I just watched them. For the first time, I felt a genuine desire not to harm them.

What happened to the ants? Well, hanging out with Buddhists can teach you a lot of creative things. I had heard Buddhists say that if they cleaned the crumbs off the bench, avoiding the ants, the ants would eventually go away. I did this and, voilà, the ants went away. Finding cockroaches and mice in the house brought similar issues. Whereas, in the past, I'd happily liberated them from their sad animal existence, now I catch them and release them outside.

Something had switched in my brain and, 16 years after I started practising mettā meditation, I still cannot deliberately or with full consciousness kill or cause harm to any animal.

I don't think the change in my brain was a religious or spiritual phenomenon. I didn't have any supernatural revelation, nor did I experience any ecstatic experience. Instead, the frequent wish for all beings to be well, happy and free from suffering reset my conditioned mental boundary of me versus others.

Before, I had viewed myself and my clan as distinctly different from others, but the mettā meditation allowed me to think and feel that everyone, including those I don't like, is just like me. The change was more than an intellectual shift in perception. It became a felt experience deep in my gut. Deep inside me, I believe that everyone is like me and that everyone else just wants the same things in life: to be free from suffering, to feel safe, to be content, to be happy and to be at peace.

The Ajahn Brahm method

Ajahn Brahm provides a variation on the above approach. He suggests that instead of using the same phrases each time, try to be creative. Tailor the phrases to suit the person or animal to which you are wishing kindness.

For example, if you are wishing kindness and happiness to your mother, you might say, 'May your joint pains subside, may your anxieties about Dad ease, may you sleep better and may you feel loved by people around you.'

If you are wishing kindness to your pet cat, you might say, 'May you feel warm and secure, may no dogs attack you, may no kids annoy you, may you have lots of cuddles.'

Tonglen meditation

Tibetan Buddhists, who I consider to be the world experts on compassion meditation, use the Tonglen technique.

Tonglen meditation, also known as 'taking and giving meditation' is similar to the mettā meditation, which uses various objects of meditation – a loved one, yourself, a neutral person, a disliked person and the rest of the world.

Practise Tonglen meditation

Start by sitting comfortably, with a straight but relaxed back.

Close your eyes.

Each stage should last for a few minutes.

Stage one

Pay attention to the breath coming in and the breath going out.

When you are distracted by thoughts, images, or sounds, just acknowledge them, remain relaxed, and go back to the breath.

Imagine a person you love or someone who cares for you deeply sitting in front of you.

Visualise their suffering, anxiety, pain, insecurities and anger as black smoke.

Breathing in, visualise the black smoke entering your body.

Breathing out, visualise white smoke exiting your body. This is the smoke of kindness and compassion going towards the object of your meditation.

Let the white smoke envelop them as they sit before you.

Stage two

Imagine yourself sitting in front of you.

Visualise your suffering, anxiety, pain, insecurities and anger as black smoke.

Breathing in, visualise the black smoke entering your body.

Breathing out, visualise white smoke exiting your body.

This is the smoke of kindness and compassion going towards yourself.

Let the white smoke envelop the vision of yourself that sits before you.

Stage three

Imagine a neutral person sitting in front of you.

Visualise their suffering, anxiety, pain, insecurities and anger as black smoke.

Breathing in, visualise the black smoke entering your body.

Breathing out, visualise white smoke exiting your body. This is the smoke of kindness and compassion going towards the object of your meditation.

Let the white smoke envelop them as they sit before you.

Stage four

Imagine a person you dislike sitting in front of you.

Visualise their suffering, anxiety, pain, insecurities and anger as black smoke.

Breathing in, visualise the black smoke entering your body.

Breathing out, visualise white smoke exiting your body. This is the smoke of kindness and compassion going towards the object of your meditation.

Let the white smoke envelop them as they sit before you.

Stage five

Imagine all the beings in the world in front of you.

Visualise their suffering, anxiety, pain, insecurities and anger as black smoke.

Breathing in, visualise the black smoke entering your body.

Breathing out, visualise white smoke exiting your body. This is the smoke of kindness and compassion going towards the object of your meditation.

Let the white smoke envelop them as they sit before you.

Random mettā wishes

One of my favourite short and sharp mettā meditation practices is shooting random wishes. This is a fun meditation that is best done if you are walking outside in nature, maybe at the park or the beach. Of course, you can also do it in a mall or a building, or even in a vehicle.

While walking in the park, look for creatures you can target, say a butterfly, a bird, or a person. If it's a person, it is best to be discreet and not stare at them!

Once you have found a target, in your mind, see that they are exactly like you. Remember that both of you want the same things. Wish them safety, freedom from pain and suffering, food, water, love, peace and contentment.

. . . .

Hack 49: When dealing with difficult people, remember that they are probably suffering, stressed or fearful.

. . . .

I suggest doing this random kindness wish to people who appear (superficially) different from you, people who are usually outside of your social, professional or family circle.

The mental change brought by regular mettā meditation becomes obvious to me when I deal with difficult, annoying or angry people. Every time I encounter them, after the initial negative reaction of annoyance or upset, my minds flips to saying, 'Tony, you are occasionally like that yourself.'

Remembering that I can be like them often does the trick, and my negative emotional state shifts to feeling soft and open.

When that doesn't work, I shift to a powerful phrase that is guaranteed to soften my heart. In those cases, my internal mantra is: 'They are obnoxious because they are suffering.'

I know that if they were not suffering and were content with their lives, they would behave differently. Shifting my attention from their surface emotional state to noticing their deep turmoil softens my heart.

At a recent medical convention, where I shared various kindness and compassion techniques to doctors, one surgeon shared a real nugget. He told me that, based on his clinical experience, the angriest and most difficult patients he encountered were those who were fearful or scared. Instead of focusing on their anger, he addresses their fear and, invariably, his patients calm down.

When we recognise that other people's anger is a sign of internal distress, we shift our position from wanting to fight back to acknowledging that the person is suffering. From a recognition of suffering, kindness and compassion can come forth.

· ·

Hack 50: When you feel you are running out of
compassion, check for compassion blocks.

· ·

There will be plenty of times when you can't feel compassion.
Don't be disheartened. That is part of being human. Things that
prevent you from feeling compassion are known as compassion
blocks.

In a scientific study of compassion among medical doctors,
we found that factors inside and outside the doctor can
significantly impede compassion. Factors inside the doctor
include feeling stressed, burnt out, depressed and fatigued.
When doctors run out of juice, compassion is in short supply.
Despite their best intentions, they end up being cold, clinical,
detached and cynical to patients.

Factors outside the doctor can include the level of support
they get, the amount of paperwork and bureaucracy they have
to deal with and issues like bullying and the atmosphere of their
workplace. These same factors apply to everyone.

You want to be kind and compassionate to family, friends
and strangers. However, if you are stressed, rushing and
lacking sleep, chances are you will find it hard to be kind and
compassionate. For busy parents, it is perfectly normal not to
feel compassionate towards your kids all the time.

The compassionate response is to acknowledge that you are
tired, spent and in need of rest. To be compassionate also means
getting the necessary support from others, including family,
friends and support agencies.

Your environment also matters. You might want to be kind and compassionate to people at work, but bullying and discrimination in the workplace make it difficult as both your stress levels and defences will be up.

If your partner is ignoring you or your children are disrespectful towards you, these issues must be addressed constructively as part of your desire to be kind and compassionate to them.

It is a myth, however, that one must be soft to be kind and compassionate. If you see your young child about to cross the street, while playing on the phone, a compassionate response might involve yanking them forcefully to safety and telling them off for not looking before they cross the road. In this scenario, talking to your child softly with extra kisses might not keep them protected. A bit of forceful love will keep them safe. That is compassion.

Sometimes, kindness and compassion require a backbone and a tough skin. Being kind and compassionate does not mean that you become doormat.

Know suffering

In 2012, Lama Zopa visited New Zealand. A Tibetan Buddhist monk, he was born in the Mount Everest region in 1946. He went on to establish an extensive network of compassion-related projects throughout the world, including feeding thousands of monks daily in South India for the past few decades, freeing animals from captivity and establishing meditation centres and hospices. He was compassion personified.

Around the time of his visit, I had started my PhD studies on medical compassion. My Buddhist friends told me that I should attend one of his public meetings because of his renown and wisdom.

I was interested in meeting him mainly from a selfish perspective. If he truly was an expert in compassion, surely, I could pick his brain for answers to one of my key research questions: 'How can we increase our compassion?'

I had done an extensive literature review on the topic of compassion, so I believed that I knew a lot about it already. Part of me felt that Lama Zopa would not add anything to my vast knowledge of compassion, and that perhaps he would just reiterate what I already knew.

At the event, which was held in a small hall, there were only about 30 people and Lama Zopa was just a couple of metres away from me. He seemed half awake, half asleep.

During the open forum, I raised my hand and stood up. 'Lama, how can we enhance compassion?'

This drew some chuckles from the crowd. Asking a Tibetan Buddhist master a question about enhancing compassion is akin to asking Stephen Hawking to tell us his thoughts on the universe.

Lama Zopa gazed at me intently. I sat down, still waiting for a response.

A devotee beside me whispered, 'He is reading your mind and doing a file check to see what you know and what you don't know.'

A few seconds felt like forever.

'Know suffering.'

That's all I remember him saying – those two words were not mentioned in any of the scientific and philosophical treatises on compassion that I had read. The phrase still rings in my head when I think about compassion.

What does it mean?

Suffering is the most important topic addressed by the Buddha. From my perspective, to 'know suffering' is to reflect on our past sufferings, unexpected challenges, pain and difficulties. These are times when we have felt rejected or misunderstood, times when we have experienced anxiety, loss or humiliation. In those times of our past suffering, what we needed was compassion.

To know suffering means to recognise that other people have also suffered or are suffering – and they too need compassion.

To know suffering means that all of us, including other creatures, experience suffering.

As we all experience suffering, we are all in the same boat and all of us need compassion from each other.

After we have experienced some significant adversity, we tend to be more understanding of others who are in a similar situation. This occurred to me after one particularly challenging time in my life that made me kinder to failing students.

I have always considered myself lucky when it comes to academic assessments or tests. I have done well in most of them, but in my academic life, I have had one unforgettable traumatic experience. I failed one examination miserably.

In the US, after training in psychiatry as a resident doctor, we had to sit written and oral examinations known as the 'boards', which were organised by the American Board of Psychiatry and Neurology.

I helped organise the review sessions for my residency group at the University of Pennsylvania. I coordinated with the various teachers and academics to make sure we would all pass. I passed the written component with little difficulty.

After passing the written examinations, I had to sit the

oral exam, in which candidates were expected to interview a patient in front of a panel of examiners. After the interview was a question-and-answer session.

I interviewed a young man with what appeared to be schizophrenia and, having had so many patients with schizophrenia and having practised multiple times with our teachers, I felt confident that I had passed with flying colours.

A few weeks after the examination, I got a letter saying that I had failed my oral examination. I was livid. How could they fail me? Most probably my examiners were 'just' community psychiatrists who were not used to Ivy League–trained psychiatrists. They had clearly made a mistake. Probably they were racist, as obviously I was not white!

After a few days on the emotional roller coaster of anger, grief and disbelief, I tried to reconstruct what had happened in the examination.

The young man had been difficult to interview. He had barely looked at me. Every time I asked him a question about his condition, his symptoms or his past diagnosis, he said there was nothing wrong with him. All I got from him was that he had been taking an antipsychotic, haloperidol. I did not have much to go on to make a proper diagnosis and work out a treatment plan.

My fatal mistake in the examination was my certainty and cockiness that this man had schizophrenia. I should have considered various possibilities. I should have had a comprehensive plan to gather more information. I made the fatal mistake of making assumptions without good grounds. It dawned on me that if I had been the examiner, I would have failed myself too. Though I managed to pass my oral examination the following year, I was devastated at the time.

My traumatic failure, and subsequent suffering, changed how I deal with medical students who fail their assessments. In the psychiatry department, we have ensured that all oral examinations are video recorded so that we can ensure fairness. If students do not do well in the process and fail, I sit with many of them, provide coaching and ask them to re-sit the exam the following month. I tell many of them that I failed the biggest examination of my life and here I am now teaching the same subject. My past suffering has transformed into present-day compassion.

The idea that past suffering or adverse human experiences increases kindness and compassion has recently been studied by Professor David DeSteno and his colleague Daniel Lim from Northeastern University. Their research showed that experiencing severe past adversity predicts compassionate feelings for those in need.

Big or small, traumatic or just annoying, we have all experienced pain and suffering. We have all experienced illness, we have all felt alone and misunderstood, and we have all felt anxiety or uncertainty. Irrespective of who we are or what we do, being human, with this body and mind, conditions us to suffer. When we accept pain and suffering in ourselves, we acknowledge what it is to be human.

We are all in this together and we all deserve compassion.

One final bonus hack: The Dalai Lama reminds us, 'If you want others to be happy, practise compassion. If you want to be happy, practise compassion.'

Epilogue

You made it this far – congratulations! Or maybe you've skipped ahead to see what's at the end – that's okay as well. I am happy that you are still reading the book.

You might be asking yourself what to do with all the hacks you've just been given. The answer is keep it simple. Putting these hacks into practice is no different to learning a new instrument or sport, so just stick with one thing at a time.

When I had my first swimming lesson as an adult, my coach told me to focus on keeping my body straight. I expected more. I wanted to learn to freestyle well. I wanted to learn how to breathe, kick and use my arms properly on day one. He insisted, 'Just keep your body straight, while you use a snorkel and fins, and worry about the others later.'

Just as his suggestion to me was to start by doing something simple and achievable, my suggestion to you is to start with something fun and easy. I humbly suggest that you choose generosity. Start small by sharing food, buying treats, spending time and giving attention not only to people you like and know, but also to others who you might not normally spend time with. Talk to strangers and be interested in what they have to say. By doing this, you are giving the gift of presence and attention.

When you give, do not expect anything in return. Give cheerfully. I can almost guarantee that once you get bitten by the generosity bug, there will be no return.

Once you've mastered generosity, perhaps look at developing kind and honest speech, then add in the other precepts.

If you want to challenge yourself further, start with a few minutes of mindfulness meditation. Even a couple of minutes a day can yield more than doing big bursts every few weeks.

Like any normal person, if there is one – remember, we are all crazy! – your interest and motivation will come and go. This is no different from trying to get physically fit, so do not let your motivation and emotions decide for you. Decide to meditate regularly. Perhaps you could join a like-minded group, for example, a regular meditation group in your local community, and remember it doesn't have to be a Buddhist meditation group.

There are also numerous online meditation groups, including those from Ajahn Brahm's monastery in Australia or Ajahn Amaro's monastery in the UK. It is amazing to me that anyone can now listen to, join in and even ask questions of these amazing Buddhist masters, whereas I had to go to Nepal, Burma and the UK to meet highly renowned teachers.

I do hope you have had a few laughs along the way or gained a different perspective on how others view life and its challenges as you've read this book, but now I have to say goodbye. A common way Buddhists say goodbye is to wish the other person 'mettā' or loving kindness.

That will be my wish for you and those you love.

Epilogue

May you be free from suffering and anxiety.

May you be happy.

May you be content.

May you be at peace.

Endnotes

Prologue: There should be more to life

page

3   *interviewed the Dalai Lama*: Dalai Lama, & Cutler, H. (1998). *The Art of Happiness*. New York: Riverhead Books.

Chapter 1: The pursuit of happiness

page

15   *A 2023 report*: Centers for Disease Control and Prevention. (2023). 'U.S. Teen Girls Experiencing Increased Sadness and Violence'. Retrieved from https://www.cdc.gov/media/releases/2023/p0213-yrbs.html.

Chapter 3: Living harmlessly

page

64   *The Zen master Thích Nhất Hạnh*: Thích Nhất Hạnh. 'The Five Mindfulness Trainings'. Retrieved from https://plumvillage.org/mindfulness/the-5-mindfulness-trainings.

Chapter 4: Precept one: kind and honest speech

page

67   *'Mastering our minds begins with mastering our mouths'*: Venkatesh, K. (2018). 'How to Practice Right Speech Anywhere,

Anytime, and With Anyone'. *Tricycle: The Buddhist Review.*
Retrieved from https://tricycle.org/article/practice-right-
speech-anywhere.

69 *lie an average of 15 times per day*: Thomason, S. (2021). 'New
research shows most people are honest — except for a few'.
UAB News. Retrieved from https://www.uab.edu/news/
research/item/12398-new-research-shows-most-people-are-
honest-except-for-a-few.

72 *'The tongue is a boneless weapon trapped between the teeth'*:
Gunaratana, H. (2001). *Eight Mindful Steps to Happiness: Walking
the Buddha's Path.* United States: Wisdom Publications.

Chapter 5: Precept two: harmlessness
page
83 *'All tremble at violence ... nor cause another to kill'*: Buddharakkhita.
(2015). *Dhammapada: A practical guide to right living.* Singapore:
Awaken Publishing and Design.

85 *homicidal fantasies*: Kenrick, D. T., & Sheets, V. (1993).
'Homicidal fantasies'. *Ethology and Sociobiology*, 14(4), 231–246.

85 *thoughts are brief*: Reynolds, J. J., & McCrea, S. M. (2017).
'Spontaneous violent and homicide thoughts in four homicide
contexts'. *Psychiatry, Psychology and Law*, 24(4), 605–627.

89 *Our morality is imposed from within*: Tisdale, S. J. (2020). 'A Life
in Her Hands'. *Tricycle: A Buddhist Review.* Retrieved from
https://tricycle.org/magazine/buddhism-and-pet-euthanasia.

Chapter 6: The remaining precepts
page
92 *If you lose your wallet*: Park, William & Airth, Johanna.
(2020). 'Why Japan is so successful at returning lost

property'. Retrieved from https://www.bbc.com/future/ article/20200114-why-japan-is-so-successful-at-returning-lost-property

92 *70 per cent of employees*: Wimbush, J. C., & Dalton, D. R. (1997). 'Base rate for employee theft: Convergence of multiple methods'. *Journal of Applied Psychology*, 82(5), 756.

95 *The experience of sexual abuse*: Chen, L. P., Murad, M. H., Paras, M. L., Colbenson, K. M., Sattler, A. L., Goranson, E. N., . . . Prokop, L. J. (2010). *Sexual Abuse and Lifetime Diagnosis of Psychiatric Disorders: Systematic Review and Meta-analysis*. Paper presented at the Mayo clinic proceedings.

95 *one in five women*: National Sexual Violence Resource Center. (2015). Statistics about sexual violence. Retrieved from https://www.nsvrc.org/sites/default/files/publications_nsvrc_ factsheet_media-packet_statistics-about-sexual-violence_0.pdf.

97 *1000 visitors*: Fight The New Drug. (2023). 'How Many People are on Porn Sites Right Now? (Hint: It's a Lot.)'. Retrieved from https://fightthenewdrug.org/by-the-numbers-see-how-many-people-are-watching-porn-today.

99 '*Sex is like brushing your teeth. It's a good thing to do but not so good to do it all day long*': Cash, Eugene. (2004). 'No Part Left Out', *Inquiring Mind*, 20(2). Retrieved from https://inquiringmind. com/article/2002_20_cash_no-part-left-out/#:~:text=Ajahn%20 Chah%20described%20battling%20with,almost%20 overwhelmed%20me.%20.%20.%20.

99 '*Both are necessary to establishing and maintaining a successful family*': Talbot, M. (2014). 'The Joy of No Sex'. Retrieved from https:// tricycle.org/magazine/buddhism-celibacy-joy-no-sex.

104 *problems with alcohol*: Center for Substance Abuse Treatment (2001). *Substance Abuse Treatment and Domestic Violence*.

Treatment Improvement Protocol (TIP) Series, No. 25. HHS Publication No. (SMA) 12-4076.

104 *alcohol were associated with violence*: Felson, R. B., & Staff, J. (2010). 'The effects of alcohol intoxication on violent versus other offending'. *Criminal Justice and Behavior*, 37(12), 1343–1360.

104 *Long-term use of alcohol*: Sontate, K. V., Rahim Kamaluddin, M., Naina Mohamed, I., Mohamed, R. M. P., Shaikh, M. F., Kamal, H., & Kumar, J. (2021). 'Alcohol, aggression, and violence: from public health to neuroscience'. *Frontiers in psychology*, 12, 699726.

104 *cocaine, cannabis, opioids and methamphetamine*: Smith, P. H., Homish, G. G., Leonard, K. E., & Cornelius, J. R. (2012). 'Intimate partner violence and specific substance use disorders: findings from the National Epidemiologic Survey on Alcohol and Related Conditions'. *Psychology of Addictive Behaviors*, 26(2), 236.

104 *cocaine, cannabis, opioids and methamphetamine*: Brecht, M. L., & Herbeck, D. M. (2013). 'Methamphetamine use and violent behavior: user perceptions and predictors'. *Journal of Drug Issues*, 43(4), 468–482.

104 *'A noble disciple …'*: Bodhi, B. (2005). *In the Buddha's Words: An Anthology of Discourses from the Pali Canon*. Boston: Wisdom Publications.

105 *'The one who drinks this brew … freedom from fear, hostility and oppression'*: Kawasaki, K., & Visakha, K. (2013). 'Jataka Tales of the Buddha Part III'. Retrieved from https://www.accesstoinsight.org/lib/authors/kawasaki/bl142.html.

105 *Buddha's precept on intoxicants*: Ajahn Amaro (Email: 9 August 2023).

108 *one cookie*: Casey, B., Somerville, L. H., Gotlib, I. H., Ayduk, O., Franklin, N. T., Askren, M. K., Jonides, J., Berman, M. G., Wilson, N. L., Teslovich, T., Glover, G., Zayas, V., Mischel, W., Shoda, Y. (2011). 'Behavioral and neural correlates of delay of gratification 40 years later'. *Proceedings of the National Academy of Sciences*, 108(36), 14,998–15,003.

Chapter 7: Generosity
page
114 *Suppavasa*: Bodhi, B. (2005). *In the Buddha's Words: An Anthology of Discourses from the Pali Canon*. Boston: Wisdom Publications.
115 *'neither the gift … completed the perfection of generosity'*: Thubten Loden, G. A., & Loden, T. (1993). *Path to enlightenment in Tibetan Buddhism*. Melbourne: Tushita Publishing.
116 *perfected generosity*: Shipman, R. (Email: 12 July 2023).
117 *the natural flow of life*: Rose, M. (2003). 'The Gift That Cannot Be Given'. Retrieved from https://tricycle.org/magazine/gift-cannot-be-given.
117 *study of vampire bats*: Wilkinson, G. (1990). 'Food sharing in vampire bats'. Retrieved from https://www.scientificamerican.com/article/food-sharing-in-vampire-bats.
118 *sharing nuts*: Krupenye, C., Tan, J., & Hare, B. (2018). 'Bonobos voluntarily hand food to others but not toys or tools'. *Proceedings of the Royal Society B: Biological Sciences*, 285(1886), 20181536.
118 *suppression of the synchrony*: Dal Monte, O., Chu, C. C., Fagan, N. A., & Chang, S. W. (2020). 'Specialized medial prefrontal–amygdala coordination in other-regarding decision preference'. *Nature neuroscience*, 23(4), 565–574.

119 *'Does making a commitment to give generously make participants happy?'*: Park, S. Q., Kahnt, T., Dogan, A., Strang, S., Fehr, E., & Tobler, P. N. (2017). 'A neural link between generosity and happiness'. *Nature Communications*, 8(1), 15964.

120 *oxytocin*: Zak, P. J., Stanton, A. A., & Ahmadi, S. (2007). 'Oxytocin increases generosity in humans'. *PloS one*, 2(11), e1128.

121 *recounts a story*: Master Sheng Yen. (2009). 'Rich Generosity'. Retrieved from https://tricycle.org/magazine/master-sheng-yen.

123 *In giving the gift of presence*: Fernando, A., Rea, C., & Malpas, P. J. (2018). 'Compassion from a palliative care perspective'. *New Zealand Medical Journal*, 131(1468), 25–32. Retrieved from https://www.nzma.org.nz/journal.

127 *'As we understand this truth'*: Rose, M. (2003). The gift that cannot be given. Retrieved from https://tricycle.org/magazine/gift-cannot-be-given.

Chapter 8: The benefits of generosity
page

129 *A group of scientists in Canada*: Dunn, E. W., Aknin, L. B., & Norton, M. I. (2008). 'Spending money on others promotes happiness'. *Science*, 319(5870), 1687–1688.

131 *good looking*: Konrath, S., & Handy, F. (2021). 'The good-looking giver effect: The relationship between doing good and looking good'. *Nonprofit and Voluntary Sector Quarterly*, 50(2), 283–311.

137 *Boston College study*: Wood, G. (2011). 'Secret fears of the super-rich'. *The Atlantic*, 24.

138 *'Greed is the salty water ... source of increasing torment'*: Ricard, M. (2010). 'Generosity (and Greed) Introduction'. Retrieved from https://tricycle.org/magazine/generosity-and-greed-introduction.

138 *a symbol for relinquishing or giving up*: Rose, M. (2003). 'The gift that cannot be given.' Retrieved from https://tricycle.org/magazine/gift-cannot-be-given.

143 *One small act of charity*: Unno, T. (2003). 'Three Grapefruits'. Retrieved from https://tricycle.org/magazine/three-grapefruits.

Chapter 9: Mindfulness

page

152 *taming of a wild animal*: Bodhi, B. (2005). *In the Buddha's Words: An Anthology of Discourses from the Pali Canon*. Boston: Wisdom Publications.

155 *Joseph Goldstein's concept*: Goldstein, J. (2013). *Mindfulness*. Sydney: St Martins Press.

164 *helping many conditions*: Khoury, B., Sharma, M., Rush, S. E., & Fournier, C. (2015). 'Mindfulness-based stress reduction for healthy individuals: A meta-analysis'. *Journal of Psychosomatic Research*, 78(6), 519–528.

165 *mindfulness-based interventions*: Goldberg, S. B., Tucker, R. P., Greene, P. A., Davidson, R. J., Wampold, B. E., Kearney, D. J., & Simpson, T. L. (2018). 'Mindfulness-based interventions for psychiatric disorders: A systematic review and meta-analysis'. *Clinical psychology review*, 59, 52–60.

165 *mindfulness benefits those with physical illnesses*: Grossman, P., Niemann, L., Schmidt, S., & Walach, H. (2004). 'Mindfulness-based stress reduction and health benefits: A meta-analysis'. *Journal of Psychosomatic Research*, 57(1), 35–43. doi:10.1016/S0022-3999(03)00573-7.

165 *Mindfulness enhances attention*: Tang, Y.-Y., Hölzel, B. K., & Posner, M. I. (2015). 'The neuroscience of mindfulness meditation'. *Nature Reviews Neuroscience*, 16(4), 213–225.

165 *emotional regulation*: Ibid.

165 *default mode network*: Killingsworth, M. A., & Gilbert, D. T. (2010). 'A wandering mind is an unhappy mind'. *Science*, 330(6006), 932. doi:10.1126/science.1192439.

165 *mindfulness practice dampens down the activity*: Tang, Y.-Y., Hölzel, B. K., & Posner, M. I. (2015). 'The neuroscience of mindfulness meditation'. *Nature Reviews Neuroscience*, 16(4), 213–225.

166 *relationship between mindfulness and telomere length*: Schutte, N. S., & Malouff, J. M. (2014). 'A meta-analytic review of the effects of mindfulness meditation on telomerase activity'. *Psychoneuroendocrinology*, 42, 45–48.

Chapter 10: How to develop mindfulness
page

169 '*Here a monk ... I breathe out short*': Bodhi, B. (2005). *In the Buddha's Words: An Anthology of Discourses from the Pali Canon*. Boston: Wisdom Publications.

186 '*To my mind, the idea that doing dishes ... in touch with life*': Thích Nhất Hạnh. (2018). 'Memories from the Root Temple: Washing Dishes'. Retrieved from https://plumvillage.org/articles/memories-from-the-root-temple-washing-dishes.

190 *after a negative emotion is triggered*: Cavazos, S. (2016). 'Schools combine meditation and brain science to help combat discipline problems'. *The Education Digest*, 82(1), 10.

Chapter 11: Building your mindfulness muscle
page

200 *a recent study of 668 university students*: Woodlief, D. T. (2017). *Smartphone use and mindfulness: Empirical tests of a hypothesized connection. (Doctoral dissertation).* University of South Carolina.

Chapter 13: Unshackling from our addictions
page

222 *develop the skill of knowing*: Carlos, M., & De la Paz, C. (2022). *Saffi Squirrel: Renee's Ginormous Bag.* Manila: Oak and Orca.

226 *less materialism or greed*: Froh, J. J., Emmons, R. A., Card, N. A., Bono, G., & Wilson, J. A. (2011). 'Gratitude and the reduced costs of materialism in adolescents'. *Journal of Happiness Studies,* 12, 289–302.

226 *less materialism or greed*: Lambert, N. M., Fincham, F. D., Stillman, T. F., & Dean, L. R. (2009). 'More gratitude, less materialism: The mediating role of life satisfaction'. *The Journal of Positive Psychology,* 4(1), 32–42.

227 *Gratitude exercise*: Greater Good Science Center. (2023). Gratitude Journal. Retrieved from https://ggia.berkeley.edu/ practice/gratitude_journal.

Chapter 14: Kindness and compassion
page

244 *some research on compassion satisfaction*: Gleichgerrcht, E., & Decety, J. (2013). 'Empathy in clinical practice: How individual dispositions, gender, and experience moderate empathic concern, burnout, and emotional distress in physicians'. *PLoS One,* 8(4), e61526. doi:10.1371/journal.pone.0061526.

246 *external stress on compassionate behaviours*: Darley, J. M., & Batson, C. D. (1973). '"From Jerusalem to Jericho": A study of situational and dispositional variables in helping behavior'. *Journal of Personality and Social Psychology*, 27(1), 100–108. doi:10.1037/h0034449.

249 *help relatives*: Burnstein, E., Crandall, C., & Kitayama, S. (1994). 'Some neo-Darwinian decision rules for altruism: Weighing cues for inclusive fitness as a function of the biological importance of the decision'. *Journal of Personality and Social Psychology*, 67(5), 773–789. doi:10.1037/0022-3514.67.5.773.

249 *seen in primates*: De Waal, F. (2010). *The age of empathy: Nature's lessons for a kinder society*. New York: Three Rivers Press.

249 *feel connected*: Cialdini, R. B., Brown, S. L., Lewis, B. P., Luce, C., & Neuberg, S. L. (1997). 'Reinterpreting the empathy-altruism relationship: When one into one equals oneness'. *Journal of Personality and Social Psychology*, 73(3), 481–494. doi:10.1037/0022-3514.73.3.481.

249 *share their values or interests*: Goetz, J. L., Keltner, D., & Simon-Thomas, E. (2010). 'Compassion: An evolutionary analysis and empirical review'. *Psychological Bulletin*, 136(3), 351-374. doi:10.1037/a0018807.

249 *kinder to those who are like us*: Bloom, P. (2017). 'Empathy and its discontents'. *Trends in Cognitive Sciences*, 21(1), 24–31. doi:10.1016/j.tics.2016.11.004.

Chapter 15: Exercising kindness and compassion
page
256 *The Dalai Lama states*: Vreeland, N., & Lama, D. (2008). *An Open Heart: Practising Compassion in Everyday Life*. Boston: Little, Brown.

273 *The idea that past suffering*: Lim, D., & DeSteno, D. (2016). 'Suffering and compassion: The links among adverse life experiences, empathy, compassion, and prosocial behavior'. *Emotion*, 16(2), 175–182. doi:10.1037/emo0000144.

Epilogue

page

276 *Ajahn Brahm's monastery in Australia*: Buddhist Society of Western Australia. bswa.org.

276 *Ajahn Amaro's monastery in the UK*: Amaravati Buddhist Monastery. amaravati.org.

Acknowledgments

I cannot thank enough the amazing teachers I have learned from over the past 20 years: His Holiness the Dalai Lama, the many Buddhist teachers from the Thai Forest Tradition (especially Ajahn Amaro, Ajahn Brahm, Ajahn Jayasaro and Ajahn Sumedho), Thích Nhất Hạnh, Bhante Gunaratana, Joseph Goldstein and many others. In New Zealand, Venerable Amala Wrightson, Russel Shipman, Venerable Sumana Siri and teachers from the Auckland Buddhist Centre. They inspired me to be a better, kinder and less-overthinking human. Their peaceful and compassionate lives motivated me to write this book and share the practical gems taught by the Buddha to non-Buddhists. Lastly, I want to thank the Buddha for his life hacks that lead to peace, happiness and contentment.

I would not have finished writing this book without the guidance and close support of the HarperCollins crew – Alex Hedley, Rachel Cramp and Nicola McCloy. Thank you for trusting in me.